PAGAN ASTROLOGY

FOR THE

SPIRIT AND SOUL

REV. ALICE MILLER

ISBN-10: 0-86690-635-5
ISBN-13: 978-0-86690-635-7

Cover Design: Jack Cipolla

Published by:
American Federation of Astrologers, Inc.
6535 S. Rural Road
Tempe, AZ 85283

www.astrologers.com

Printed in the United States of America

In love and joy, for all my pagan friends,

With special thanks to Sara and John Shepard.

Books by Rev. Alice Miller

Principles of Astrology: Planets, Signs & Houses

Dynamics of Astrology: Interpreting Aspects

The Soul of Astrology: Inner Dimensions of the Modern Moon

The "Limits" of Astrology: Saturn for Today

Retrograde Planets and Consciousness

Nodes of the Moon

The Part of Fortune and the Astral Body

Designs for a New Age: The Grand Cross, Mystic and Other Rectangles

Heralds of a New Age: Interceptions

Possibilities for a New Age: Intercepted Planets

A Coven of Planets: A Pagan Astrology

A Kabbalistic Design of Planets: Astrology's Tree of Life

Healing the Inner Child: The Astrology of Family Dysfunction

Getting Birth Charts on Target: Techniques Old and New

FOREWORD

My life has been exceedingly eventful. Some would assign credit to Uranus on my natal chart horizon. I have used my life for experimental applications connected to my studies in astrology, psychology, and metaphysics.

My life runs on resistance and I have used crisis to kick my consciousness into increasingly wider/higher orbits. It is working well, now in my third Saturn cycle. Born a Crone (Capricorn on the fourth house cusp, the IC), I have finally reached the proper age for it.

I have enjoyed teaching and speaking before groups. The inspiration for this book came from teaching the astrology portion of an introductory Wicca class. I realized that most pagans need an astrology which emphasizes the Moon and the dynamics of polarity in the form of *masculine-feminine* relationships. This book was written to meet that need. Anyone who chooses to approach natal horoscopes in a non-traditional way will find it fun. Classically Uranian, this work applies ancient concepts in a revolutionary new way.

This is an astrology book for the visually oriented. The imagery of this book is designed to trigger your own intuitive gifts. For those who look forward to the incoming Age of Aquarius, there is a special treat in the sections on the outer planets. Each of these is projected up to that period.

I had a great deal of fun writing this book. May each of you have as much fun reading it!

Blessed be,
Starsinger, a.k.a. Alice Miller

CONTENTS

The Structure of the Coven

Recently, a great revival and expansion of Pagan traditions has occurred in America. Traditional *Christian* religions have so often failed in carrying the message of the original Christ to latter day followers that they have begun to seek enlightenment from older sources. Not all of these seekers are committed to the Pagan path. Many are simply trying to discover where Christianity made a wrong turn. Thousands have sought the origins of their belief in the earlier history of religious faith and practice grouped loosely under the banner of Paganism. The most popular of the Pagan beliefs at this time is probably Wicca.

Modern covens are dedicated to self-knowledge and the expansion of awareness that naturally arises out of it. Each serious student of Wicca must learn some method of discovering information and/or guidance from extraordinary sources through a divination technique. Like the ancient prophets, and the Babylonian Magi, many have discovered astrology. Both an art and a science, astrology is popular because it naturally leads consciousness in new directions. When the mind learns to think in nonlinear ways by working with a circular chart, it begins to experience life outside the ruts of more conventional belief systems.

Various astrological techniques are available for a variety of divinatory purposes and levels. The ancient principle of astrology is, "As above, so below." Modern astrologers add a new version, "As without, so within." The true seeker will begin to reverse these statements, realizing that, "As below, so above; as without, so within." Those who are willing to begin to look at and switch the ends of the philosophical equations naturally occurring in the patterns of astrological language easily gain mastery of the potential that lies beneath its surface. With that mastery, comes the ability to touch the stars.

This book is designed to convey meaning through image and metaphor. In it we have pictured the human personality as a coven. Using the planets as symbols for its parts, we have viewed them as persons within that coven. Each coven has its own character, derived from the persons in it. Our birth horoscope presents a picture of the inner coven in each of us. That picture gives us a blueprint for the whole being.

The Wiccan approach differs from traditional *solar* astrology in making the Moon the most significant planet. Wicca is a religion dedicated to the humanistic viewpoint. It centers on our relationship to our physical being and to our Mother Earth. It directs our inner growth toward unfoldment—more of the lunar soul than of the solar spirit. When soul makes progress, the effects will naturally be incorporated into spirit.

We define the Soul as that pattern, mold, or imprint that directs spirit into form. It empowers the spirit to accomplish its goals in form. We define Spirit as the energy-essence that is the source of life and that which takes whatever pattern Soul gives it. Body will be a physical manifestation of the process. We use the analogy of Sun as spirit, recognizing him as often being too "hot" and too "bright" to be worked with directly, so we filter his rays through the Moon. She "takes the heat" and the light and modifies or transforms it, stepping down the intensity as needed to make the processes of enlightenment and enlivenment more comfortable and understandable for physical beings living on Earth.

As described in a natal horoscope, all planetary energies are reflections of the Sun's emanations. Each is shaped and colored by the individual planets that reflect these rays. It is the Moon that re-gathers these modified rays and directs them into physical form on the Earth. We might say that we are conceived and gestated by her. Having arrived on Earth, we begin to look to our new mother, Mother Earth. This may explain the feeling, in certain highly evolved souls, of having originated somewhere other than the Earth.

Two planets lie between Earth and the Sun. These are Mercury and Venus, the "administrators" of light and of love. They give definition and separation to the two types of solar emanations that are the primary "causes" or principles of human life. Lying just beyond Earth is her "twin," Mars, the masculine polarity to her feminine nature. As the Earth is an adoptive mother to the lunar offspring, so Mars is an adoptive father to the solar component of that offspring. As Earth signifies form, so Mars signifies energy, the urge to move out, to seek individuation, to reach for emancipation.

Next come the solunar reflectors, Jupiter and Saturn. We have traditionally regarded Jupiter as male, but she is not. Hers is the principle of conception, of generous permissive bounty, of joy and laughter. She can only be a secondary mother figure. We might call her a daughter of the Moon or the Goddess of Multiplication. Saturn has been linked with Chronos as Father Time. He is that and more. Traditionally, he has been responsible for setting the limits on how far Earth-children might go, and when. He stands guard over the evolutionary process to keep it in balance. We might also call him the God of Cycles.

Beyond Saturn lie those planets that we commonly call trans-personal. We should probably call them trans-human. These are the representatives of the universal forces that call us to be more than mere members of a coven. They call us out to be High Priestess and Priest, then to merge into oneness with the Goddess and the God, and finally to dissolve into the essence of life.

First comes Uranus, the great changer and higher vibration of Mercury. As Mercury keeps the records of the coven work within one lifetime, so Uranus holds the records of all the past and future lives. He is the keeper of the Akashic Records. Then comes Neptune, the great dissolver of limits, the homogenizer. She is the love-bringer and the higher vibration of Venus. As Venus bonds individuals, allowing individual human auras to blend, so Neptune bonds group auras into consciousness groups, blending people of different races, beliefs, and cultures into greater and greater wholes.

Out of the intercourse between Uranus and Neptune comes Pluto, who is the avatar of the next age or phase. Walking in power, she is the culmination of the mating of form and formless. She can be either or neither and she signifies the end of the "human" phase of development and the beginning of the trans-human phase. The ultimate sorcerer, she can speak her word and bring universes into being.

We intend this book, in true Wiccan fashion, to be read playfully and for fun. Do not take it for a super-serious metaphysical study. Instead, play with it. Enjoy it. Let any lessons herein be learned in the pleasant way of childish simplicity. So mote it be. Let the reader have fun!

THE HIGH PRIESTESS MOON

The High Priestess of our internal coven is the Moon. She is a[1] mother-aspect and our place of origin—the womb. She is transmitter and translator of the energy of Sun/spirit. She is the soul of the coven and nurtures its spiritual growth. All energies pass through and are monitored by her.

When researching childhood in a chart, the Moon signifies our entry into life on Earth, including the body from which we emerged, she who cared for us when we were helpless, and the atmosphere and/or home of which she was the queen and high priestess. As our world expands, her role may seem to recede. The moment we begin a path of personal or spiritual development, we are required to face the original conception of life and this world that she gave us. Regardless of how we feel about her, what she was and how she related to us becomes the foundation of our consciousness. She is our glory and our despair.

Without her there is no "personal coven," and should we survive as a solitary soul, we will have no "roots," no supporting "family structure" to which we can turn for additional

---

[1]The Earth is also a mother, for she is caretaker and nursemaid. She feeds and clothes us; she nurtures our physical and social growth. Primarily, she is described by the Ascendant and the contents of the first house, as modified by the entire house structure

strength when we feel weak. Neither will we have the capacity to bond with others, joining our magical power to theirs for the completion of larger tasks. Lacking lunar connection, we cannot discover internal-friends with whom to share our joys and triumphs. When the Moon is intercepted, this will be our reality for many years. When the Moon is ruled by an intercepted planet, or poorly aspected, there will be some intermittent support but it will probably not be consistent or dependable, or not of the right kind or quality.

Each Moon sign mothers her planets in her own way. Most help them to grow into productive and happy members of the coven. Others drive their children to higher awareness along the harsh negative way. Some Moon-mothers find their fulfillment in essentially emotional nurture, some in physical nurture, some in mental nurture, and some in spiritual nurture. Each runs, or shares the running of, or ignores the running of the personal coven of personality according to her inherent nature, just as some women express their femininity in one way and others in other ways, some more and some less.

Each Moon represents a specific level of soul development and shows us how the soul integrates with body and spirit. When the Moon is ruled by one of the traditionally masculine deity planets, she will have to integrate and accept those aspects of herself represented by such planets before she can reach her full potential as priestess in the life of the individual. Ruled by the more feminine ones, she will more easily find her niche in the personality coven. Ruled by the neuter planets, she has an opportunity to develop new qualities of being.

MOON IN THE SIGNS

Aries Moon: The Mars-ruled Aries Moon must integrate and accept Mars-desire or she will be barren and inhibited in her personal and spiritual growth. Until she decides what she wants and pursues it, she can provide neither ritual nor leadership for the coven. Such covens accomplish little beyond acting as a place where the this Survivor Soul can hide and feel protected. Her glory is that when she trusts her survival instincts, picks up her courage and moves out, she becomes a true Seed-Being.

Taurus Moon: The Venus-ruled Taurus Moon is a Maiden, so she will naturally become priestess after a time of service. She must, however, be willing to "move up" when the time comes so that her service begins to be rendered—no longer in the mundane areas, as a servant—but rather through the auspices of the goddess power inherent within her. Let her mature gracefully with age, experiencing the triple-goddess pattern as she moves through life. In graceful aging lies her glory and her power.

Gemini Moon: The Mercury-ruled Gemini Moon may never really decide whether to be a solitary practitioner or to lead her own coven. She may study for a while, then look to some other belief system for a while, serve as maiden or apprentice for a while, then forget the whole thing for a while. She will probably never mature sufficiently to really rule the personality as priestess because she would rather collect ideas than formulate any real beliefs. She does not want to take the time or do the work of really developing the Soul to a place of leadership in the life of the individual. She will probably neither follow nor lead the self, but will co-exist with it as one sibling with another. Still, such individuals retain a certain child-like charm when allowed to go their own way, and may make some valuable contributions to whatever coven they choose to bless with their appearance from time to time.

Cancer Moon: The Moon-ruled Cancer Moon is the "born" priestess, being clearly named "child of the Moon." In such individuals there is a clear channel through which one or more goddess aspects flow. She will quite naturally "draw down the moon" for she is a direct heir to all the lunar goddesses in history. She was born to lead the inner coven—and, if female, an outer one. *Growing into* her role, she has great potential to become the powerful generation point for the covens of the future. Beginning life as a Mother, she may end it as a maiden, after her *children-in-consciousness* have reached maturity.

Leo Moon: The Sun-ruled Leo Moon must claim her hereditary right to rule her own life and to shine—often more brightly than her mate. She must learn to delegate responsibility to other members of the coven, becoming a queen or figurehead for the personal coven, or else she will become so scattered that she never achieves the glowing reputation which is rightfully hers. Instead, she will present a haughty and demanding appearance that interferes with the generation of group power as required for magical work. She must accept her own inner priest before she can work well with the outer one. Her glory lies in claiming her spiritual heredity and becoming the Goddess that she is.

Virgo Moon: The Virgo Moon is the more feminine of the two Mercury-ruled Moons. She may prove a very practical coven manager, but as priestess she will lack depth unless she comes to the realization that she is pure in nature and cannot be sullied by any activity. She will best function as maiden during the early years of life, during which period she may undertake an apprenticeship with the High Priestess of her coven. Like the Taurus Moon, her lineage is more Earth Goddess than Moon Goddess and she lives to serve humanity. She must let go any tendencies toward fastidiousness, get *down on the floor,* and play with her children. In doing so, she will learn much about the future of her coven. They will teach her the true nature of humility and the glory of her proud heritage.

Libra Moon: The Venus-ruled Libra Moon must function in equal partnership with her Solar Priest. When she does, they will share the coven tasks, ruling the entire self with a balance of male and female energy. All parts of the personality will then live together in harmony and without judgment. If the two have an adversarial relationship, their dysfunctional relationship will damage the children in the coven. Some Libra covens may not be as productive in manifest terms as others but they generally provide a places of peace and solace for their inner members. The glory of the Libra High Priestess is best expressed in equal partnership, and the children born of functional coven marriages are often the leaders of the next generation.

Scorpio Moon: The Pluto-ruled Scorpio Moon can wield a great deal of power so long as she remains aware that her power comes through her priest and from her coven. This is the true essence of magic. Remembering this, she can accomplish almost anything. As user and transformer of power, she is invincible, but if she begins thinking of herself as the source of that power she becomes destructive to the entire coven. She will then become a "black" witch for a time, but will soon "crash and burn." In potential, and in potency, this is the truest High Priestess of all the zodiac. She has the ability to transform her world.

Sagittarius Moon: The Jupiter-ruled Sagittarius Moon represents the broader view. She has been High Priestess for a long time and has hived off many covens so she feels no real need to fulfill this role at this time. She will become something of a Solitary but will make herself available to the local High Priestesses as an advisor and counselor. She may be invaluable to several covens while not being an official member of any of them. She is the goddess-principle personified and will protect and guide all the other aspects of being. She is wise and true. She knows when to speak and when to remain silent.

Capricorn Moon: The Saturn-ruled Capricorn Moon must claim the authority of "age." She is an old Soul and can be demanding and crotchety. She must learn to accept the patience and wisdom which are inherently hers and act in the capacity of the Crone, which she truly is. The Capricorn Soul must remember to lead, to teach by example and not to drive or demand compliance. Maintaining her dignity, she must set an example for the young Maidens to follow. Doing so, she becomes the High Priestess to high priestesses. This is her glory, her role and destiny.

Aquarius Moon: The Uranus-ruled Aquarius Moon represents what the priestesses of the future will be. Because she knows much that she cannot explain, she may simply function behind the scenes telepathically providing inspiration wherever needed. It will be she who will show how to adapt the old principles to the new times and it will be she who adds power to the possibilities of the future. She may seem to have little to do with the structure of the coven, being primarily a voice and a channel for the drawing down of the messages of the gods and goddesses. She will have little outward form except what the High Priest and the coven give her. A potent influence on the lives of all who come within her psychic domain, hers will be the unseen hand that shapes the future. She is the mother of all that will become. Quite literally, she is a direct incarnation of divinity. Like the Goddess, she is not very solid. Like the wind you can't always see her, but she makes her presence felt.

Pisces Moon: The Neptune-ruled Pisces Moon can hardly do other than become the mystical priestess that she was born to be. She may seem to have little or no power at the conscious level, but does in fact have all power at the unconscious levels where true magic occurs. She is a will-o-the-wisp, dancing in fairy fields and her priest may have his hands full keeping her from dancing right off this earth. Still, she brings beauty and peace wherever she goes as she flits butterfly-like from blossom to blossom.

THE HIGH PRIEST SUN

The High Priest of our internal coven is the Sun. By sign placement, he defines our incarnational intent. The Sun symbolizes the father, as he who gave us our family name, our place in the community, and our reputation. We look to him to help us set our goals about what we wish to grow up to be. A good High Priest stands tall, setting a good example. He will never be too proud or stiff to reach down a hand to the young or weak. He sometimes carries the little ones on his shoulders.

The High Priest's role is that of protector and partner of the High Priestess. He may also be her lover, her friend, fulfilling many roles in her life, giving her form and purpose. He is her catalyst, the quickener of her womb, and the one who goes before her to prepare the way. At different times he may be her father, her husband, her brother, her son. As the gods are to the goddesses, so the Sun/Priest is to the Moon/Priestess. When the High Priest serves well, protecting, supporting, providing the necessary stability and protection, his priestess and the entire coven will honor him. No matter how gifted she is, a priestess cannot fully use her gifts without the place, the resources, and the opportunity which he provides.

Each solar type provides for its mate and its aspect-children in its own way. Some serve best as inspiration; some are good counselors, providing emotional support; some are ready with ideas and suggestions; and some are merely the providers of material support. The best manage to be father, teacher, financial backer, and protector simultaneously, setting a "tone" or overall atmosphere in which the other aspects of being can develop.

Each Sun represents a specific level of spiritual development and the ways in which the solar energy is radiated throughout the being are a direct result of that. Some are far more committed to their priestess and their coven than others who may be natural solitaries or agnostics. When one of the more traditionally feminine planets rules the Sun, he must integrate and accept these feminine qualities into his persona before he can serve fully in the priestly role.

THE SUN IN FEMININE SIGNS

Cancer Sun: The Moon-ruled Cancer Sun can be slow to develop until he realizes that he is not so much feminine as he is *young*. Here Cancer usually represents the child, or more likely the infant, rather than the mother to whom we customarily assign it. He would better serve in the coven, as an apprentice, until he has nurtured his own sense of self to a maturity level adequate for leadership. With awareness of his youth and his need to learn and grow, Cancer will begin to mature rapidly. Notice that the youngest infants grow most rapidly. If Cancer will begin at the beginning, he may finish before those who started later in their evolutionary development.

Pisces Sun: The Neptune-ruled Pisces Sun would rather be the priestess than a priest. He is naturally gifted in psychic work, although he may have difficulty with traditional magic because his tendency to worry about ethics often delays what he could so easily do. Let him pour his talents through his partner, for he will find that they are fluid and will combine with her own to the greater good. If he will do this, the Pisces High Priest will lose distinct definition from his Priestess as spirit and soul become blended and fused. The ultimate goal of human evolution is to lose the boundaries and divisions within self. Full fusion between the two equals tremendous power, the very power to work miracles. It is true that Pisces does not see reality clearly. He can, however, create his own reality, and this he must do if he is not to lose himself.

Taurus Sun: The Venus-ruled Taurus Sun, while nominally feminine, converts to masculine use for the High Priest quite well. Only when his possessiveness toward his priestess and coven is invoked, does he become aggressive, and then he is formidable. While he will never start a fight, if someone else does, he will always win. An excellent provider, he will always see that his High Priestess and the coven have food, drink, and a place to meet. Beyond that he may retire to the background, only speaking when called upon. Gentle with little ones, he deals honorably with the older members of the coven.

Scorpio Sun: The Pluto-ruled Scorpio Sun is an extremely powerful spirit, accustomed to being in control of the personality. He holds the very power of life and death within his being. Like steam or static electricity, if not directed and controlled, it can be quite dangerous. Much as he might like to run the coven in his own way and by his own might, if he is to truly demonstrate his great sorcery he must channel this power through his lunar High Priestess. Until he learns this, his very being will exist in a state of constant tension which often produces addictive behavior. He needs a safety-valve or a ground wire. When he gives up his need to control, and becomes willing to work with his High Priestess as a team, he will discover that the merger is one of the most potent and productive around. She will give form to his massive energies. Creation will be manifest where once only destruction reigned.

As High Priest and Priestess become more completely bonded, they will discover that he can gather up the energies of the coven and channel them through her work. In this way, the magical work of the coven shows an exceptional level of potency. Healing work may be so powerful as to literally bring the ill back from the edge of death, while tangible things will multiply exponentially. The very shape and form of coven life may change, as though true alchemy were at work. It is.

Libra Sun: The Venus-ruled Libra Sun will work side by side with his Moon-partner, sharing the load equally. This placement shows spirit and soul in balance and any magical work will be the result of their cooperation. As with the Libra Moon, there will not be a strong sense of separation of roles. Each knows well that cooperation is necessary in leading a coven. Each must balance the other. This coven can expect justice. Disharmony will not be tolerated. Other planets will be expected to cooperate and to do their share in maintaining the growth and development of the personality-coven. Occasionally, when they do not, the Sun and Moon become adversaries, splitting the personality-coven apart. The key understanding is that, whatever her sign, the Moon must allow her Sun equal rights and authority in the coven, so that the coven is adequately energized and led.

Virgo Sun: The Mercury-ruled Virgo Sun will be inclined to divide the roles of Priest and Priestess rather sharply, for he wants a well-ordered personality-coven. With a dissonant Moon, this may not lead to a happy marriage or a very productive coven because magical work requires more blending of the male and female than he is willing to do. These covens are well-run and "neat," with perfect rituals which somehow lack the power which one would expect to see. Still, they provide a place in which pathworking can be sampled by many, without becoming too deeply involved. The potential of this placement is that, if the newly-perfected Virgo-spirit practices patience and cooperation with his Moon-Priestess, mastery is within his grasp.

THE SUN IN MASCULINE SIGNS

Aries Sun: A Mars-ruled Aries Sun will be a strong defender of the coven. He allows nothing and no one to interfere with his High Priestess. His attitude toward her is almost reverent and he will literally protect her with his life. Not always as good a provider as Taurus, his protective instincts must be directed toward protection of the coven from exposure and starvation. This usually does not take much effort because he is sensitive to anything that causes pain to his lady and his little ones. His own intuition is strong but often unconscious so it works well for him to direct it to and through his High Priestess. If she understands and respects him, this will be one of the most energetic covens around, and the Lunar High Priestess will be its queen.

Leo Sun: The Sun-ruled Leo Sun will often create a coven of high visibility because the High Priest has a regal air and a sense of high drama. As his queen, his High Priestess will be greatly honored—if she is not, someone will hear about it. He will not ask; he will simply tell the other members of the coven what to do, with the full expectation that they will obey. Since he has such a glowing aura and is so sure of himself, he will generally get unquestioned obedience from the coven. This makes for a very unified coven with great power and unquestioned loyalty. The Leo High Priest will not need to be a defender because his very presence is his defense. Few will dare to attack anything in his domain, so most of the power of the coven can be turned to creative work. Much that is beautiful will come out of it.

Capricorn Sun: The Saturn-ruled Capricorn Sun is from a hereditary line of witches and will wear an almost-tangible mantle of authority. He knows how a coven should be run and will delegate all of the psychic work to his High Priestess. Often neither knows how much of the power expressed in the magical work actually comes through him. He is the masculine equivalent of the Crone. Having succeeded in all his goals in prior lives, he now devotes most of his energies to the success of his heirs, always working through the High Priestess. He sets the parameters of the inner circles and moves them outward as needed to keep the coven going and growing. Meanwhile, he may appear to be doing little except "keeping the coven in line." Coven members may complain, feeling that he drives them beyond their limits with his expectations. Still, his coven will never lack for members. Only in retrospect will it be understood how great an influence he has had on everyone else.

THE GENDERLESS SIGNS

Gemini Sun: The Mercury-ruled Gemini Sun may seem to be in two or more places at once. He may do all the talking for his priestess and almost drive the coven crazy at times. Yet he has a youthful charm that keeps them more loyal to him than he seems to be to them. Seemingly all the work that gets done in this coven gets done in spite of him. He is the perpetual student and has read every book and talked to every witch he can find. In the process he has become a walking encyclopedia, but he seems not to know it. He sows ideas broadcast with no appearance of order or reason. Still, many of his carelessly cast seeds take root in just the right place to grow and produce. If his High Priestess understands him and works with him, his coven can acquire a name for being one of the best teaching covens around.

Sagittarius Sun: The Jupiter-ruled Sagittarius Sun is a great source of wisdom. He will be highly honored and respected by his High Priestess as she becomes the transmitter and translator of his wisdom. He may appear childish because he has little tolerance for solemn ritual, knowing that rituals can be boundaries to the growth and expansion of consciousness. Theirs may be a strange-looking partnership, but those who are watching it will discover that it is exceptionally productive. This happens because he channels his high levels of energy through her, impregnating her creativity. This coven will work visible and tangible magic. If it is not that, they are luckier than anyone has a right to be. Those who watch must decide, for this High Priest will never tell, being more interested in getting others to think for themselves.

Aquarius Sun: The Uranus-ruled Aquarius Sun is the priest of the future. He is, perhaps, more sorcerer than priest. Knowing how to change the shape of things, he can adapt the old ways to the new, plotting the direction of the future from the wheel-marks of the past. He is sometimes so unusual in appearance that he filters his very self-image through his High Priestess Moon. She will express a subtle feeling that often says more about him than any words he could speak or any appearance he could present. As a High Priest, he will be nearly invisible, for he stands always in the shadow of his Priestess while she seems to administer the duties of the coven. He is a nearly pure consciousness with no form except the form of whatever container (Ascendant) it is poured into. The coven may appear to be without a High Priest, the sole responsibility of the High Priestess. Still, it does amazingly well and those who watch will wonder why. Some may discover that not all fathers are visible, that the greatest protection and the finest inspiration come from the unseen realms of spirit.

The Aquarian coven is the coven of the future, a new Wicca built on the foundations of the old. Adapted from the faint memory-traces of the past, this Wicca may not look much like it did in the days of the ancient Celts. Still, it will be the place where magic returns to a world which had almost forgotten how magical its childhood was. The new covens will be covens of High Priestesses and High Priests, for all have reached the ultimate degrees of development. The future of these covens will be like the ancient past, when full internalization of the Gods and Goddesses occurred and worlds were created. As the past was, so the future will be.

VENUS: THE MAIDEN

While the Moon is the representative of the Goddess as Mother, Venus is her representative as Maiden, and in her function she is still a virgin. She is youthful and her function is to radiate love in its non-maternal aspects. She adds beauty and comfort to the coven structure and teaches it to value life and goodness.

She helps her High Priestess in the household tasks of the coven, like an older sister to the other members, and an older daughter to her Priestess. Depending on the temperament of her High Priestess, she may function as second in command, as coven manager, or merely as a servant. Sometimes she is simply an altar-girl to help in the ritual work of the coven. How effectively she can perform under the guidance of her High Priestess depends on the compatibility of temperament between Moon and Venus. When the Venus-girl-child is of an incompatible element with the lunar mother, it is difficult for the feminine teachings to flow naturally. Then Venus may have difficulty in expressing her maidenliness. If he is more available, she may turn to her Solar nature for guidance.

Ultimately her task is to provide cohesiveness and harmony within the coven and to prepare the place in which magical work will be done. This can mean seeing to the details which make ritual work possible or acting as mediator between the High Priestess and the coven members. Some maidens quietly provide sustenance and comfort from the background, while others take a more active role in coven life.

VENUS IN THE SIGNS

Aries Venus: When Venus is in Aries, the Maiden will be youthful and full of enthusiasm, and may have definite ideas of her own about how to fulfill her duties. She will probably do more than needed or required and sometimes create havoc with her enthusiasm. Still, she is such an innocent that we must forgive her. Whether she will ever settle down and mature into a proper High Priestess is questionable. But she is a delight to have around because she radiates love in a way that draws all of the other coven members together.

Taurus Venus: When Venus is in Taurus, the Maiden may still be physically youthful, but will have the temperament of someone older. She will work quietly and diligently and never miss little details. She will notice which coven members need emotional support. Quietly doing what is needed in the most efficient way, she will subtly move them to the High Priestess or help them herself. More than that, when needed, she will do the same for her High Priestess, who, if so inclined, can lean on her heavily. Sometimes she becomes the hostess of the coven because she is so gracious. Her only fault is that she is so good at her job that some High Priestesses may find her threatening.

Gemini Venus: When Venus is in Gemini, the Maiden is like a tomboy. She may be so busy playing with coven members that she forgets her housekeeping duties. Still, she keeps the communication lines open and will call the attention of her High Priestess to any problems which may be occurring in the lives of other coven members. Some may call her a gossip and a busybody, and she may be that, but it is her definition of love. Allowing her to design and write rituals might be better than expecting her to do more traditional maidenly tasks.

Cancer Venus: When Venus is in Cancer, the Maiden is definitely a Priestess-in-training. She is like a little girl playing Mama. She will be so caring and nurturing of the coven members that she may need a second Maiden to do the housekeeping tasks which are normally hers. Her only real fault is that she cannot say no to anyone. Still, if the High Priestess will be patient with her, she will mature over time, learning that love is more than merely nurture. Meanwhile, her intuitive kindness to all will excuse much.

Leo Venus: When Venus is in Leo, the Maiden is an actress and her finest performance will be helping her High Priestess in ritual work. Here she will add light, love, and considerable power to the work. She may require much praise to spur diligence in the housekeeping duties required of her. Leo does like to be noticed and given credit. Still, with the right High Priestess, one who continually encourages her performance, she can be one of the best Maidens around, a shining example of love to all. Her only fault is that she will not work without appreciation; she needs an audience.

Virgo Venus: When Venus is in Virgo, the Maiden is a worker. A natural healer, she is usually happy as an apprentice to her High Priestess. She does not really want to be anywhere but where she is, for she believes that she was born to serve. If allowed to remain in her role of secretary, servant, and nurse, she will serve long and faithfully, often without notice or reward. Her only fault is a tendency to be too much a perfectionist. She sometimes struggles between a need for perfect timing and the difficulty of always having to have the altar and the cakes arranged perfectly. This can sometimes delay the ritual work

Libra Venus: When Venus is in Libra, the Maiden is a mediator. She will develop a personal relationship with each member of the coven and will act as go-between for the High Priestess. However, she also expects to share her priestess' reputation. She can work in perfect tandem with the High Priestess if allowed. Otherwise she may become judgmental and will find a way to "get even." She must never be treated as a servant; she is an equal.

Scorpio Venus: When Venus is in Scorpio, the Maiden will often be the secret power behind the magical work of the coven. She is a tremendous energy receptor and she knows how to channel this power through the work of the Priestess. Frequently she also knows how to gather up the powers of the individual members of the coven and add them to her own. With this realization she will become either the greatest asset or the greatest liability for the existing High Priestess. When her time comes she will be one of the most powerful of the Priestesses in existence, for the good or ill of those who share her personal world.

Sagittarius Venus: When Venus is in Sagittarius, the Maiden will do much to expand the work of the coven, for she has great ability to attract energy from the environment around her. Whether for good or ill, she will magnify whatever work is being done by the whole. She will not be much interested in competing for the crown of the High Priestess. Content to teach wisdom, she is a spiritual advisor to the High Priest and Priestess. She can work with a partner, but is more apt to work alone since she has great awareness of the many facets of herself. She is more a Crone than a Maiden, but lacks the sense of dignity and restraint common to Crones. She is usually content merely to add value to whatever is being done by the whole. Her only fault is that if she comes to believe in an unworthy cause she can be as great a magnifier of evil as of good.

Capricorn Venus: When Venus is in Capricorn, the Maiden will actually be a Crone serving as Maiden. She will work with dignity and reserve and will dedicate all her efforts toward the success of the coven, including—if she feels the necessity—the impeachment of High Priest and Priestess. She is the keeper of the ancient wisdom and is potent in manifestation. She may, however, be a dogmatist and a hindrance to a free-thinking High Priestess. Since she can exert psychic power to prevent changes with which she does not agree, she can be disruptive in certain covens. Still, if given due respect and allowed to act as an advisor she will usually serve well and faithfully.

Aquarius Venus: When Venus is in Aquarius, the Maiden will know instinctively what is wanted and needed by her Priestess and the coven. She can see problems clearly and use her ancient powers as a shape-shifting sorcerer to create needed changes in the structure of the coven. She may not always be loyal to her High Priest and Priestess, but she will always be true to the principles of Wicca and to the God and Goddess. If leaders of the coven are intelligent and adaptable, she will be a great asset and the whole coven will become a place where quantum leaps in consciousness occur. If not, she will probably start a revolution, allowing the crises of such a path to resolve the issues.

Pisces Venus: When Venus is in Pisces, the Maiden will be a subtle presence, often unseen, but never unfelt. Her love will penetrate even the most defended personalities and she may be the unseen power behind the throne of the High Priestess. She is a dreamer, a visionary, and a poet. Her subtle presence can soothe the most difficult interpersonal problems that may arise. If anyone can get the lion to lie down with the lamb, it will be she. She is the pagan version of a Christed being, and affects those around her more than will ever be noticed. She seems merely to add beauty, but in truth she adds peace, harmony, wisdom, and power as well. Like any beautiful thing, she uplifts all her fellows. Her only weakness is her inability to defend herself. If attacked she may abdicate from the coven and lose herself in a world of dreams.

THE MAIDEN'S WORKING PARTNER: MARS

In the coven is a young man who squires our Maiden around. He is her working partner, her lover, and defender. Whatever she needs, he wants her to have and will do what is necessary to get it for her. Although there is no such recognized position, his role in her life is quite similar to that of the High Priest in the life of his Priestess, except that being "young," these two are not "married." They are still in the courtship stage. Because this is so, their relationship is often more intense and less committed. There is a kind of tension between them that is both creative and destructive. Passion—whether based on love or hate—is the most potent, life changing power in existence.

The magical power produced by this relationship can be more erratic than that of their role models. The Mars-Venus couple may experience greater peaks and valleys in the levels of their passion. Sometimes they have not discovered how to make that passion creative. Magical energy surrounds these two, but, with a marked difference in their evolutionary levels, much of it may remain unmanifest potential. The more her needs mesh with his desires, the more he wants to give her what she needs, the more potent their relationship.

Where the work of the coven is concerned, much of his effectiveness will depend on her level of awareness. As always, the feminine gives form and purpose to the energies of the masculine. It matters not how much he brings to her if she does not see a need, or a use, for it. When this occurs the output of Mars becomes energy with no goal, or anger. Anger can still be converted to determination if Mars is highly evolved but his will be a hard, uphill road if Venus does not recognize her need for him.

For a steady dependable working partnership, it is best if Mars and Venus are in the same element. This gives them the kind of advantage which is conferred by similar cultural and religious or philosophical backgrounds in people. It makes their relationship more harmonious. They can devote more of the energy generated from the relationship to constructive projects and less to efforts to communicate sufficiently for real cooperation.

When they are in opposing elements like air with fire or earth with water, the relationship will work either very well or very badly. This will depend on how much awareness the coven has. If fire understands that without air he cannot burn and air realizes that only the heat of the fire can cause her to expand (in consciousness), this couple has great potential. Their path may not be smooth, but, from time to time, it will produce spectacular results. Similarly, if earth understands that water is necessary to his fertility and water understands that earth can give her the form and stability she lacks in herself, they too can "be fruitful and multiply."

When they are in an inconjunct or quadrate relationship, they must overcome difficulties through effort before they can learn to communicate and/or work together. Earth and fire may grow little, but from the combination beautiful ceramics can be created. Water may extinguish fire, warm it to make soup, or create steam for an explosion or an engine. Air and earth can create a dust storm or become a perfect environment for a fire. Sometimes a gust of air is required to get stale earth aerated and active. Water in air can be fog; it can also provide a place for the greening of life.

MARS IN THE SIGNS

Aries Mars: Mars in Aries is in his element. He is energetic, eager, fearless, and will go anywhere to get what he sees as desirable. If necessary, he will go to new lands (of awareness) to please his lady and meet her needs. His only weakness is that he, literally, does not see her as separate from himself. While he is getting what he *thinks* she needs, she may be doing without what she truly needs. If they are not well matched, she will have to find a "need" or use for what he brings. Otherwise she must convince him to pause long enough, and listen intently enough, to discover what it is that she really needs. This can take years and delay their magical work for a long time.

Taurus Mars: Mars in Taurus moves very slowly and deliberately, and may not seem himself at all. Still, he is thorough and always finishes what he starts. If his lady understands and appreciates him, his desire to be needed can be channeled into an increasing level of power output. He has more energy than he appears to, but he refuses to waste it on projects which he considers worthless. If in compatible signs the couple will produce steady, dependable, ongoing results and their work will be quite spectacular for its sheer volume. If incompatible, sometimes the capacity for destruction is equally spectacular. Then the Priestess and Priest must learn to use "controlled explosions." Sometimes they can harness them and make an engine, but it will take real ingenuity.

Gemini Mars: Mars in Gemini may scatter his energies all over the place, and he is seldom a faithful lover. He cannot feel desire, so he thinks it instead. As a result he questions everything, even the necessity of having a lady-love in his life. His attention span is not long, so most of his goals must be short-term. If his lady is relatively evolved, and if she understands the value of words and ideas in the creative process, she may be able to take what she needs from the myriad of things he brings, creating something from them. In this way, she can probably give meaning to his words and ideas and extract wisdom from them.

This Mars will work better in the future than it has in the past for it refers to the energy contained in words and ideas. As we learn more about the role of consciousness in the creative process, the effectiveness of Mars in Gemini will increase. At present he is still problematic and seldom mates well with his Venus. Still the pair may have fun and sometimes play is more creative than work. Occasionally such a couple will generate great magical power "by accident"—and probably never realize that they have done so.

Cancer Mars: Mars in Cancer depends heavily on his Venus for form and structure. Here desire is "in flow" and will take the path of least resistance, as does water. If Venus is more conscious, if she knows what she needs, then she can provide the necessary structure to channel the Mars energy. The wise Venus encourages him, lifting his spirits sufficiently high to produce a waterfall effect. This generates a more concentrated force. If she can match her needs to his abilities, deferring some of them, his energy levels will rise with maturity. Without her help and cooperation, Mars in Cancer often finds his energy dissipating without direction. This creates "Much ado about nothing."

Leo Mars: Mars in Leo is proud of his ability to get what his lady needs, but he expects her to have good taste and to appreciate him. He is so attractive that she usually finds a way to make whatever he gets for her fulfill her needs, even if it means changing her role within the coven. As a result he may inspire her need to train for leadership of the coven, if only to make her lover proud. Remember that if life takes its natural course, the day will come when the Priestess retires and the Maiden should be prepared to step into her place. Young Mars in Leo looks forward to that day and will be very frustrated if his lady does not see the need to move up. Because of this, Venus needs will often be upgraded to a more enlightened level by a Mars Leo.

Virgo Mars: Mars in Virgo is a tireless worker. Without a more relaxed Venus to modify his energies, he will often become a workaholic. More a craftsman than a magician, his real desire is to serve and to be useful. With a good working partner who can appreciate his technical abilities, he will develop magical hands which energize all that he touches. The pair will then become excellent additions to any healing work which the coven does. With a more spirited Venus who does not understand the benefits of a precise methodical approach, his efforts may produce little more than friction. He will constantly "spin his wheels."

Libra Mars: Mars in Libra wishes to share equally with his Venus. He works harder or relaxes more, depending on the natural vibratory rate of his lady, adapting for a harmonious and creative relationship. Some magic which comes from this pairing is not terribly useful, but all of it will be beautiful. Understanding that will be important for their Priestess. In its own way, beauty *is* useful. Either way, the two will provide a harmonizing and moderating effect on the personal coven. Depending on the overall makeup of the coven, this may increase or decrease its creativity but either way this coven will provide a pleasurable experience for the members involved.

Scorpio Mars: Mars in Scorpio is like steam, hot and fluid. He will need a strong Venus with the ability to recognize the needs to which such great power can be applied. This Mars has an almost inexhaustible supply of energy, for he has the capacity to store and contain his desire to intensify its release. If his lady enjoys high levels of energy, if she can recognize critical needs and direct his energy toward them, this pair can produce an exceptionally high quality of magical work. Occasionally it produces the power to rejuvenate or resurrect what is aging or dying. With a shallow or unwise Venus, this Mars will perform destructively, like the steam boiler that explodes.

Sagittarius Mars: Mars in Sagittarius will dance and play and generally enjoy life, for his energy is enthusiasm. He is generous to a fault and needs a Venus who's needs take a shape that is compatible with his energy flow, which seems to rise and fall with the tides. Thus she must be able to order the priority of her needs and be ready to catch him at floodtide for the more significant ones. During the ebbtide they may merely explore their relationship and determine the strategy for the next energy surge. If she can match her need-pattern to his energy pattern, if she is flexible, they can expand a little into a lot. This brings "good luck" to the coven.

Capricorn Mars: Mars in Capricorn is a prodigious worker because he has a wise and mature comprehension of the efficient application of energy. He may, however, limit his use of energy to projects which he considers worthy of his notice. He needs a Venus that can deal with his tendency to be miserly or one who can charm or tease him out of it. As he matures and becomes less judgmental and less concerned with his public image, he will become a more effective power source in the personal coven. His desires are the best guides to the true purpose of the coven. He needs a Venus who recognizes the significance of allowing the desire nature to lead and who will make him the true head of her life. If she will do this, she will discover that what he wants will always be what she needs. This can be a true win-win situation for all. If she does not, it produces a stalemate.

Aquarius Mars: Mars in Aquarius will project his energy far into the future. If his working partner, Venus, is also farsighted, they will work exceptionally well together. It will be as though the coven has a fairy godmother granting all their wishes and manifesting all that they hope to achieve. The possible difficulties here are fairly obvious. If Venus is unwilling to change, insisting that she needs what she has always needed, Mars can do little for her. The Venus who is adventurous, open to possibilities, will do well with this Mars because he can reach out into the future and bring back the *impossible*. This is a very potent and extremely knowledgeable Mars but he cannot—or perhaps will not—produce anything he knows is not needed, useful or desirable.

Pisces Mars: Mars in Pisces is wispy and dreamy. His power comes from his dreams. To be productive, he must work with a Venus who is willing to see the need for dreams or one who recognizes the power of the subconscious. This Mars works automatically, without conscious attention, producing whatever Venus feels that she needs, whether it serves any purpose in her life or not. Woe to the unwise need system when a Pisces Mars is her champion for his high abilities will actually drown a hedonist in her own requests. It is easy to see that this Mars is the best or the worst, depending entirely on his mate, Venus.

MERCURY: THE FETCH

In the history of Wicca there has sometimes existed an official position named "The Fetch." Although usually a male, gender plays no real part in the performance of his duties. He is publicist and communicator, liaison to other covens, and generally in charge of getting messages from here to there. Because he is in contact with all members of his own coven, with representatives of other covens, and of the non-Wiccan public, he is often a great source of ideas.

The Fetch has two aspects. He also creates and manages memory files, serving as coven historian. Whether or not we give him the official position as Fetch, every coven needs a member who is willing to serve in this way. His name is Mercury.

Mercury serves best when he is not too strongly gender oriented because he needs to relate and to communicate with both masculine and feminine. He must be unbiased and willing to exchange ideas with a wide range of value and belief systems. His function is to explore ideas and experiences, learning from the exchange of information and experience. In a sense he is also doorkeeper and guardian of the circle, allowing or refusing entrance to those who seek entry to it.

MERCURY IN THE SIGNS

Aries Mercury: Mercury in Aries will probably fetch more than you want or need. He is childlike, an enthusiastic communicator, and sometimes so busy talking that he forgets to listen. However, his enthusiasm and his great desire to be the very best at what he does will drive him to curb this tendency. He becomes increasingly efficient as he matures. Meanwhile, his energetic approach to whatever he does gets massive amounts of work done. If not required to follow a too-rigid rule-book by an overzealous coven leadership, he has the capacity to handle a myriad of details. However, his method of sorting may look more like a centrifuge than a filing system, so he needs great latitude and as little interference as possible.

Taurus Mercury: Mercury in Taurus will be quite serious about her duties as Fetch and will see that all ideas of value are communicated promptly. She sorts incoming information, keeping only what she thinks is valuable. Her housekeeping is immaculate, with files less massive than some others, but well-ordered and easily found. She is extremely practical and sometimes insists on fixing things that do not need fixed. Occasionally the message delivered loses some of its meaning in the interests of good grammar or good manners. At her best she brings practicality to a new level, for she knows that the natural tendencies in life make the best and most efficient methods of operation. She is the ultimate pragmatist.

Gemini Mercury: For better or worse, Mercury in Gemini can be like having two Fetches. If both decide to talk at the same time, communication can get garbled. However, with proper guidance and instruction from the coven leadership, one will act as messenger and the other will handle the practical details of secretary-treasurer to the coven. Often a walking encyclopedia of information for the rest of the coven, he has difficulty drawing conclusions, making any judgments or choices, or accomplishing much on his own. Without good support from his planetary coven, the Gemini Mercury will look like ideas scattered to the winds. To those who would criticize, we would remind you of the many plants who produce seeds equipped to be scattered on the winds.

At his worst, the Gemini Fetch is a gossip and a trouble maker, for he sometimes uses no judgement about whom he tells what. At his best, he is a seed-man, bringing new life, not only to his own coven, but to the world. He is a true light-bringer, for his mission in life is to gather as much information as possible and to make it available to as wide an audience as possible. Generally, when we turn to thank him for his services, we find that he has already gone.

Cancer Mercury: Mercury in Cancer is fluid, like mind in flow. If she fetches at all, it is when the mood strikes her. She follows the path of least resistance, going through what she cannot go over, going around what she cannot go through. She is not always on time, because she may meander through the fields of thought. However, given time, she always arrives where she is needed with the information requested. We cannot hurry or entirely control her, but she never goes dry. Always, no matter how old she may be, her words and her ideas flow forth to those who thirst. When the more energetic members of the coven have burned up or burned out, she will still be pouring out her rich treasures of thought. She is the true intuitive, a pure channel for the ideas of the ages, and a great treasure to her coven.

Leo Mercury: Mercury in Leo is bright, dramatic, and creative. He does not fetch in the ordinary way. Instead, he shines his wisdom like a great light, or a billboard, and expects whoever wants the information to watch for his displays. Pay attention and you will probably learn something. Ignore him, you will probably learn something as well, but it may not be what you wanted! Still, if given free reign and the recognition he seeks, he will be an excellent creator of ritual. His rituals will be elegant, and intolerant of change. Leo must be taken at face value, even if the face is a mask hiding a trickster. He is the true Samhain child, and will only play tricks on you if you refuse his treat. Pet him and praise him. Then he will purr like a cat and do anything you ask him to do.

Virgo Mercury: Mercury in Virgo, is the best or the worst of Fetches, depending on coven leadership. She is like a teenager, perfected in form, with the "body" of an adult but little experience in adult matters. She needs clearly stated instructions about what information is needed by whom. We must give these instructions tactfully, being sensitive to her feelings, knowing when to parent her and when to treat her as an equal. If allowed to assume increasing levels of responsibility in ways that give her more successes than failures, she will become an efficient business manager, secretary, and social director for the coven. Her great gift is efficiency and if allowed time to practice her newly acquired skills without pressure she will give outstanding service to the personal coven.

Libra Mercury: Mercury in Libra will fetch only if treated as an equal by clan leadership. He will not serve, but he will share in the work of the coven. If approached in a democratic way, he will remain committed to the best interests of the coven. Given this, he is a communicator par excellence. Conversation is his forte. In this context he will make an elegant messenger. He will know exactly who requires what information. At his best, he is a mediator and peacemaker, having a gift for seeing and stating many points of view and finding the common factors within them. At worst, he is opinionated, judgmental, and set on getting even. Listen to Mercury in Libra and grant him due respect.

Scorpio Mercury: Mercury in Scorpio will re-form the role to suit herself. She is an excellent detective and will discover the deepest and most hidden thoughts behind any conversation. Her ability to ferret out a secret is uncanny. She can coax and persuade the coven into a unit of power for coven pathworking. She can also blackmail her way into coven leadership. Thus, this Mercury can be the best friend or the worst enemy of the coven and its leadership. In this position, she will surely discover the full meaning of the witches' rule of three. Whatever she does, for good or ill, will react directly into her own life and being. If it is good, let her accept the benefits with grace; if it is difficult, let her not allow rage to compel her to something even more destructive.

Sagittarius Mercury: Mercury in Sagittarius will give the principle of communication a new application. He does not wish to be bothered with contacting many people. Instead, he sets up a network so he can notify A, who will notify B, who will notify C, and so on. As for contact with the outside world, his style will be that of a public relations person. He knows what information is publishable and where to have it printed to reach those individuals or groups to whom it is directed. He also knows that this method sometimes reaps rewards not predicted or expected. The work of this coven must be understood and dedicated to the greater good. For good or ill, this Fetch will broadcast it to the world, offering the opportunity, for personal growth, and for influencing the public.

Capricorn Mercury: Mercury in Capricorn is not so much a Fetch as she is a walking archive. She knows the history of the coven, its traditions, its successes, and its failures. Understanding what works and what does not, she also knows the value to be extracted from experience, so she will rarely interfere, even with a poorly lead coven. Still, if her advice is asked, she is quite willing to share the bounty of her age and wisdom. This Mercury is more Crone than Fetch, and is an excellent consultant who's talents sometimes get wasted by her dedication to doing what has always been done. This can leave her disgusted and depressed. Should this happen, she will be more likely to say, "I told you so," than to offer constructive suggestions. She can be a great asset to the coven, but leaves it up to the coven whether they will avail themselves of her wisdom and experience. Make her the business manager of the coven. In this role she will shine and so will her coven.

Aquarius Mercury: Mercury in Aquarius is the messenger of the future, and he brings to his coven, the winds of change. Wherever this Mercury is, the coven will either revolutionize the meaning of magical work or end up in rebellion. This gives the Aquarian reputation for being either genius or insane. Clairvoyant, his message service is from the God and Goddess to the coven. In the traditional sense, he is no fetch at all. Still, in the cosmic sense, he is just that. Sometimes we cannot see him at all, for he is a shape-shifter, taking on whatever form serves his purpose as messenger of the gods. His knowledge is so extensive that he must often slip it into life "sideways" because the local and general consciousness cannot recognize an idea, except they believe it possible. Sometimes he is "fairy godmother" granting a long held wish that has finally accumulated enough energy to manifest.

Pisces Mercury: Mercury in Pisces will not only flow like her Cancer sister; she will float and drift and enter the wispy world of dreams. Do not send her to fetch anything; she will forget what you sent her for. Instead, let her bring what she wills, for a guiding presence pervades her thoughts. It gently pushes her here and pulls her there, like a breeze moving the clouds about. This Mercury may appear totally devoid of logic in her methods. Still, if you do not force her to use rigid guidelines, you will be amazed at how often important information arrives just when you need it—and it will be a very logical solution when examined after the fact. She is timid and easily hurt. She will try to do whatever is asked of her, and feel guilty if she cannot. Shouting and pressure will simply make her too nervous to produce anything, but quiet trust and expectation will bring miraculous results.

JUPITER: MERCURY'S PARTNER

This working partnership is a non-sexual one, and the potential for creative power that exists within it is just beginning to reach the general awareness. It is the power of in-form-ation, where ideas define an area where belief can create. This couple's power comes from Jupiter's understanding of the many-faceted nature of Mercury consciousness.

As the sciences of psychology and sociology emerged on the scene, a (meta)physics of mind was born. Studying the interaction of Mercury-Jupiter and its connection with Neptune allows us to move far beyond the beliefs of the past. We can then discover the magic-with-out-ritual which is the natural direction of development from the rich heritage of the Wiccan past. It also allows us to move beyond superstition, into the conscious and intentional use of ritual as a tool. Jupiter links ideas into concepts, revealing the meaning of relationships and life. She is the principle of growth which, added to consciousness, becomes creative.

At one time Jupiter ruled both Pisces and Sagittarius, both faith and beliefs. The two were indistinguishable. Faith then demanded unquestioning acceptance of the unexplainable. For many it still does, but as the Piscean age dissolves into Aquarius, a new idea is spreading. Moving into the area of consciousness where we can accept it as a tenant of belief, it gathers force. We have developed a rational explanation for how faith works and why dreams come true. Understanding how to separate facts from truth, we can learn more about the dynamics of life in this universe. The true work of Jupiter has begun. Our horizons are exploding outward, because we have looked inward.

We may say that Jupiter acts as society's representative in the personal coven. She holds the key to our belief systems, for she represents the social climate in which our coven exists. As such, she shapes our use of language, defining what is and is not possible. To the extent of her enlightenment, she binds or frees Mercury to ask the questions to expand our beliefs, our world, our universe.

As Mercury is the outer voice speaking to society, so Jupiter is the inner voice of society that talks back to us. Some would call her the inner Parent. If that Parent and the society it represents insists on following a narrow and rigid belief system, our Mercury/Fetch is limited to conveying only the information that will pass through the narrow gates of our beliefs. If that Parent and the society it represents encourages us to explore, investigate, and expand our awareness, Jupiter will become the great enlightener through her ability to calculate conclusions and infer principles from the available perceptual information. Later, in the more evolved signs, through the auspices of Mercury, she will also have use of Neptune's memory function. Together, the three planets act as an internal computer that puts its outer expression to shame. As Jupiter and Neptune move through the signs, that computer speeds up.

To understand the full capacities of the Mercury-Jupiter partnership, we must recognize Mercury's capacity to mutate from a perceptual function to a tuning function. As Mercury moves forward from Libra through Pisces, Jupiter increases her scope. The ability of the more highly evolved Mercury placements increases her data base exponentially. Eventually the human consciousness can and will surpass all its known parameters, moving beyond the solar system, beyond the galaxy, into the very heart of Eternity where the symbol of ritual becomes the reality of creative action.

JUPITER IN THE SIGNS

Aries Jupiter: Jupiter in Aries identifies with a truth or a belief. Much depends on the inquisitiveness of Mercury here. The parental voice is a loud one, and personal beliefs are a projection of the parental belief system. This Jupiter has so few doubts about why she is on Earth and what she is to do, that she may not hear Mercury's questions. The gift of the placement is that, above all, this Jupiter believes in survival. In time her belief in self and in life usually turns her around, causing her to look inward for the seed-truth she carries.

When the question of survival or self-realization arises, the answer is in the identification. This Jupiter must live or die by her beliefs, and she wants to live.

Taurus Jupiter: Jupiter in Taurus values her beliefs as she values her life. Requiring the body to be sacrificed to the soul, the parental voice is a threatening one. It condemns all physical pleasure, making it a great sin. While this masquerades under the label of rabid Christianity, it probably has a karmic past in the East, with its wandering beggar-priests. The gift offered by Mercury's questioning is the realization that if the body is a home for the spirit, it must be a temple in which our Goddess lives. How then can it be so misguided and sinful? Finally, Taurus' practical loving kindness will set her free to care for her physical temple and to bring the gifts of profit and pleasure to the personal coven.

Gemini Jupiter: Jupiter in Gemini thinks about beliefs, talks about beliefs, and continually questions them, seeking for meaning behind the words. Early in life he has at least two parental voices in his head and they constantly argue about what is true and how things work. Gemini Jupiter may spend years trying to make sense of it all, as each answer leads to another question and truth is some distant star that urges him onward. It can be said that he has a mathematical mind. His greatest gift is that his beliefs will never become limits on his life, because he will keep on asking more questions, reaching for more answers.

Cancer Jupiter: The Moon-ruled Cancer Jupiter has rather childlike beliefs, bonded into her by her mother. They are fluid and dominated by her emotions. Thus she will be resistant to any questioning by Mercury. She will follow any authority figure who makes an impression on her, allowing him to define her path. Still, any planet in Cancer must and will grow. In time Cancer Jupiter will mature into a more definite shape for Mercury to examine. If his questions *feel right* to her, she may then begin a real journey to maturity. Much will depend on the relationships between Jupiter, Saturn, and Mercury. Wherever the path of least resistance, there you will find Cancer Jupiter, watering the surface of life or penetrating to its heart.

Leo Jupiter: The Sun-ruled Leo Jupiter is activated but immature. Having inherited his beliefs, he may pretend to a wisdom he does not possess. Still, he has the charm of a child playing "let's pretend" games and can act his way through most situations. The gift of this is that in taking on the role of wisdom he very often taps his own genetic resources, activating the brilliance that is his birthright. If Mercury will present him with proper data, he can create miracles of enlightenment and growth in the lives of others. Only if Mercury is introverted[2]

---

[2]Retrograde or in one of the very personal signs, such as Aries or Taurus.

will he learn as much as he teaches. This proud Jupiter may take over the Solar role, hiding the Sun behind his large presence. When he does, natives are more identified with Consciousness than Spirit, Soul, or Body.

Virgo Jupiter: The Mercury-ruled Virgo Jupiter may be so fastidious about her beliefs as to deny Mercury's questions or ideas. Her belief system is a hands-on project that has little time or patience for the diversity of Mercury. A Mercury incompatible by sign can accomplish little except a collection of experiences that seem irrelevant to the path of growth. When the planets match by sign or element, the coven can become so formalized and ritualistic as to discourage thinking. When they are too dissimilar, they may never learn to cooperate at all. Sometimes visual or hearing losses result. Virgo is adolescent, and Jupiter placed here can be so set on holding the *perfect* belief system that she limits her own growth process. With time/Mercury and practice/Virgo, a new perspective on life can create a better relationship between the senses and the mind. Virgo's hands hold the key to mastery. The question is, "Will she use it?"

Libra Jupiter: The Venus-ruled Libra Jupiter has learned the value of cooperation. Her most significant belief is in the union of two or more. She believes in societal structure and is prepared to share her wisdom through Mercury's communication function. Her ability to do so depends on Mercury's sign. When placed in air or fire, Mercury is naturally talkative, and the combination may produce an *evangelist*, out to convert society to her views. When he is in earth, his hands-on approach must learn to cooperate with her tendency to *waste time* in talking everything through. A water Mercury may flood Jupiter with too many sensations during his youth, but will grow into a true partnership as his channeling abilities develop. Libra Jupiter can channel great wisdom.

Scorpio Jupiter: The Pluto-ruled Scorpio Jupiter is truly fused with Mercury. Here, thought naturally calculates concepts and principles as wisdom or slyness. This placement shows the *natural witch*. Great passion is attached to her beliefs, empowering them. This coven can be a power in the community and/or a powerful creator of good. Occasionally, with too much stressful experience early in life, that power channels into paths of destruction. Someone must pull the weeds from the garden of life, and Scorpio Jupiter can be the messenger of reformulation and social change. At certain levels these covens become political units with considerable power to change their world. Jupiter is the planet of natural expansion. When fused with Mercury, words have great power. For better or worse, this Jupiter is truly larger than life.

Sagittarius Jupiter: Jupiter is at home in Sagittarius, able to travel far and expand her influence. Only when Mercury has learned the *wrong language* in which to convey her wisdom, can she be limited in her outreach. This Jupiter functions like a high-speed computer and her natural gift for language will lead her to a place where she can understand and be understood. Sagittarius Jupiter is born with a large stock of wisdom stored in memory/Neptune. The only necessity is recognition of the Mercury key she holds in her hand. When that is difficult, a new location can provide the information she needs to unlock her own store of wisdom.

Capricorn Jupiter: Jupiter in Saturn-ruled Capricorn is limited only by her belief in the current definition of human possibilities. If she understands herself as an evolutionary being, she can be the most successful teacher in the zodiac. When she does not, she will teach her own limits. Still, the maturity inherent in Capricorn Jupiter naturally takes leadership of the inner coven, leading it down the spiritual path and beyond the old Capricorn definitions. Because Jupiter is about expansion, placement in Capricorn can do no more than slow the progress, requiring a step by step process. Each new fact that Mercury brings to her, each memory he calls up from Neptune's realm, moves the coven a bit higher. Gradually the formal application of concepts becomes Jupiter's greatest power, her brilliance and glory, her genius. Jupiter in Capricorn becomes the power behind the scenes of life and society. Always she produces growth in self and others.

Aquarius Jupiter: Jupiter in Uranus-ruled Aquarius enters life as *more than human* understanding. Here the cosmic principles naturally expand every part of life. Every planet in the coven can benefit from her inspiration and genius, provided they are not too fixed or stolid. Any Jupiter-Uranus connection gives ability to use astrology as a divinatory language.[3] Understanding comes by inspiration. More accurately, the conceptual (Jupiterian) language of astrology understands the Uranian realm of galaxies and stars at the request of a curious Mercury.

Whatever is placed in Aquarius lives *between the worlds* and has access to them both. This Jupiter placement permits the Mercury perceptions to compare the inner life and outer circumstances. Astrology's theme, "As above, so below," acquires real meaning. We could say that this Jupiter moves into the galaxy, where she can draw data from both Earth and Cosmos. Her calculations produce conclusions about the very nature of LIFE and of the Universe. The rapid advance of computer technology is a clear symbol of the rapid expansion of human awareness.

---

[3]Ed. note: The author has a Jupiter-Uranus tredecile.

Pisces Jupiter: Jupiter in Neptune-ruled Pisces almost disappears. When planets enter Pisces, they lose definition, becoming merged into the whole. This placement moves us from one who *has* understanding to one who *is* understanding. We understand the nature of life without learning to, or trying to, and we live our lives from that understanding without realizing that other people do not have this capacity. No longer students, we become teachers-by-example, the living expression of the new phase of humanity. No longer *learning animals*, we are now *learned animals*—or perhaps we can no longer be called animals at all. Instead we have become the true sons and daughters of the Goddess. On the more mundane level, we no longer *have* computers; we *are* computers. More than High Priest or Priestess, we are the human expression of God and Goddess. We do not *call down* the Moon or Sun, because our every word is theirs.

SATURN: THE TRADITIONALIST

Historically, Saturn has been a father figure, but not a kindly one, for he was the disciplinarian and boundary-setter of the personal coven. He represented the "laws"of life as they provided limits on human behavior. Meant to change and expand as people matured, they were like the rules set for children not yet able to judge the extent of their abilities.

Until the discovery of Uranus, Saturn was the outermost planet. He held absolute authority, insisting that the old beliefs represented the law, beyond which we could not go without falling off the Earth into the pits of hell. Wherever a belief system becomes rigid and stagnant, wherever it threatens its followers with punishment for departures from the beliefs of the past, there sits a grouchy old Saturn. Often pictured like Cernunos, who ruled the old religions that the then-modern Christianity supplanted. Today many Christian churches are as obsolete as the new converts of centuries past judged the old mother-religions to be.

Today a new version of Wicca is arising from the ashes of the past. Although based on the old principles, modern Wicca has been adapted for use in a world vastly different from the one where the principles originated. Any belief system that is going to prove its worth must be a living, growing one. It is just because so much of Christianity is dying in obsolescence that the Wiccan revival has occurred.

It is unknown whether the ancient Wiccans understood the principles by which ritual practices worked; we assume not. This can explain Saturn, who was once simply the keeper of traditions. He told us what worked and what did not and his words became moral laws. When Christianity came along, he did the same for it. Sometimes he threatened consequences, sometimes karma, sometimes hell.

Thus, for many of us, Saturn represents our fears and may wear the costume of an overactive conscience. We might also call him the Lord of Superstition, for he holds us to promises no longer valid and keeps us stepping over cracks in the sidewalk long after we know better. He represents the urge to think of ourselves as imperfect and in need of refinement and he relates to the philosophical addiction for pain that pervades the consciousness. Always he limits and binds; most of all he limits joy. He will continue to do so until Uranus steps in with her broader vision and points out that we must always link Saturn's rules to time. Each rule is for a particular period of development and when that period ends, new limits must be set.

In an expanding world, with a deeper awareness of the nature of consciousness, Saturn teaches us to sort sensory input for perception. He allows us to focus our sight or hearing or another sense to a particular point so that we may think and learn. In the personal coven he keeps us on the subject at hand until we have completed the task. He reminds us that there are times for work and times for play. He also rules the very principle of the circle we cast, for it is a boundary, used for a time, then let go.

The modern coven will study the ancient ways and have great respect for them, using them as guidelines in creating their own new traditions. Wicca, being a religion of the Earth, is a religion of life, and life ever changes. Both time and space have expanded since the old days; as a result we have given to Saturn the role of keeper of the traditions that were and to his mate Uranus the role of keeper of the possible traditions that can be. Let him rule time and let her rule space, and let them stand opposite Sun and Moon, as advisors to the coven.

SATURN IN THE SIGNS

Aries Saturn: Saturn in Aries identifies with the old ways. He can be a loud-mouth bully or the voice of an abusive parent. Sometimes this keeps the coven in a childish mode, not allowing the natural process of maturation. Such a coven can become a snobbish social club that creates little magic because magic is change and no change is allowed.

The redeeming quality of Saturn in Aries is the urgent need for the coven to survive. This may trigger a rebirth of the pioneering instincts. Much will depend on cooperation from

Uranus, and her ability to transform him from a panicky, abusive, father to a wise grandfather.

Taurus Saturn: Saturn in Taurus is a miser, often so conservative of the coven's resources that little real work gets done. He will evaluate, and evaluate, and evaluate each project, taking so long to get started that he has earned a reputation for being lazy. Still, when he finally starts something, we may be sure he will finish it, if only because he will not allow us to waste the resources invested. This holds true, even when giving up the project would have been better. He is slow to start because he knows that once started he must finish. He cannot let go. Neither can he forgive. If his Uranus is to do anything at all with him, she must use drastic means to get his attention. Consequently, the only transformation possible to Saturn in Taurus is usually crisis that threatens his life or his livelihood. To him it is the same thing.

The redeeming quality of this placement is that in the end he values the coven and its work so highly that he will do whatever is necessary to preserve it, even if he has to change his whole lifestyle.

Gemini Saturn: Saturn in Gemini wears two faces. Some of his internal laws are rigid and unbending. Around these he will be a harsh disciplinarian, allowing no leniency to transgressors. Others are so lax as to be almost without form, serving as little more than guidelines. The coven with this Saturn will be forward looking and active in some areas, while remaining hidebound and stubborn in others. This may create a living dichotomy, a personality split, and/or a pragmatist who questions other people's motives but never his own.

The grace of this placement is that this Saturn is rather youthful, and he can realize it. He wishes to learn. As he matures he may recognize the true knowledge of Uranus and, with her leading, he can realize how irrational holding such inconsistent beliefs is. At this point a transformation can occur in the coven and its whole personality will change. The characteristic split of Gemini will then stand as past and future, and the coven will have won its wisdom the hard way.

Cancer Saturn: Saturn in Cancer makes feelings law. He will follow his instincts, whether they seem to make sense or not. Generally this works well if he has enough self-knowledge to be able to sort his feelings from those around him and especially those who set up his earliest emotional responses. Because instinct is a form of reasoning which processes information at or above the speed of light, good instincts allow for unusually rapid growth in consciousness.

When the bonding process has been damaged, Uranus will have her work cut out. Still, the grace in this is that like Gemini Saturn, Cancer Saturn is still quite young. Whatever is in Cancer must by definition be born or reborn and this birth implies some rapid growth as the newly born or reborn go through an infancy stage. Here, Uranus serves as midwife and caretaker to the new growth. She acts in her capacity as friend, and out of her great love for all that lives.

Leo Saturn: Saturn in Leo thinks he is king, and woe be to any who would cross him. He expects to be both star and director in his own life drama, and he will be so, even if he has to play a failure. Ruled by the cycles of the Sun, he is either up and shining or down and dark. Bright Leo Saturn will coax the coven along with his shining warmth and much will be accomplished during this phase. If all does not go well, if other members of the coven do not meet his expectations, dark Saturn will appear, sulking, spreading gloom, and making the whole coven so miserable that they will wish that they had or could follow his dictates.

The grace in this placement is that at the break of each new day the sun forever rises and with it the sun-worshiping Saturn. An adaptable Uranus will know when to catch him in the creative mode and inject her inspiration at those times when he is most likely to succeed. This can keep the Leo Saturn pacified and radiant far into the night, so that summer seems to last forever.

Virgo Saturn: Saturn in Virgo is a hard worker. Sometimes he makes hard work of things that could be done in far easier ways. Still, he finds merit in suffering, for his law requires him to earn his rewards, often by struggling to perfect methods that are obsolete. He does not seem to realize that spending great quantities of energy in learning to build a perfect campfire is not particularly useful to one who lives his entire life in a New York apartment. He may tell you that for sixteen generations the men in his family have been famous for their ability to lay perfect campfires and he has no intention of letting his ancestors down.

Uranus will have a difficult time with this Saturn. Frequently she has to set fire to his apartment on the theory that if he is building a home, he cannot build fires at the same time. This technique works to the extent that he becomes fully involved in home-building. But then he may be starting a new tradition that he will expect his sons and grandsons to carry on. Still, she knows that each generation is less fixated in the past than the last, so perhaps she may as well let him do things his way.

Libra Saturn: Saturn in Libra is ruled by the law of relativity. He constantly weighs this "law" against that "rule," and he is commonly known as a pragmatist. He will go by whichever definition of life permits him to fit into society best. Believing in society, he believes in marriage as social necessity and he will always look to others for confirmation of his limits. In modern society we see many people who are married and will stay married at all costs, even the cost of his own Soul.

The grace in this placement is that, at its best, Libra Saturn represents the law of love and he will put the good of others before his own. This may allow his Uranus to convince him that allowing certain others to leave his life is in their best interests. Later, when a little time has passed, he will discover that is was for his own good as well.

Scorpio Saturn: Saturn in Scorpio refers to a fusion of law and power. Often during the early years his life will be held hostage by certain (usually moral) laws that brought instantaneous retribution upon the luckless child who transgressed them. There will be, then, no separation in consciousness between these laws and his sense of purpose. If other factors in his internal coven urge him toward spirituality, he will be unable to think of this in any terms other than those defined by the authorities in his childhood. This can require him to put so much energy into keeping control of his own feelings, ideas, etc., that he begins to look and feel like a pressure-cooker overfilled with steam. It can make him just as dangerous, for to survive, the steam has to be vented off somewhere. He will then be subject to raging at those who love him most. If he is lucky he will drive them away before activity occurs which brings the wrath of social law down on his head.

Wherever we find Scorpio in any personal coven there is a fusion in consciousness that needs to be made conscious. Here something was forced into the developing sense of self, in a way that required it to be regarded as an absolute. Because of this there will always have to be some type of transformation in this area, either because it has exploded the coven or because it threatens to.

At its best, Saturn in Scorpio refers to the laws of transformation, to the principles of growth and evolution. At its worst, if refers to the tendency in human consciousness to resist change and use the tension of life in a self-destructive way. Here, Uranus has her work cut out. How easy or difficult the process is will depend much on her ability to teach and move him.

Sagittarius Saturn: Saturn in Sagittarius refers to concept of law and to the tendency for social law to expand until it limits the freedoms it was intended to preserve. With this placement the real danger to the coven and to society is that laws may multiply to the point of meaninglessness. When the web of laws is so excessive as to make every person a lawbreaker, respect for the law is lost and civilization breaks down. We see this daily in news reports.

With so many laws, we have no hope of living within the law, and people, especially young people, are giving up the pretense of doing so.

Wherever we find Sagittarius, a tendency for things to multiply or expand conceptually and/or exponentially follows. If the laws of the internal coven do this, it will become incapable of movement. Unless Uranus intervenes, the coven will begin to regress toward disintegration and death.

The grace of this placement is that at its best, Saturn in Sagittarius refers to the laws of consciousness. Natural optimism and joyousness often break up the seriousness of the coven. When this occurs, space is made for the wisdom lying at the heart of Sagittarius to expand. A good Uranus can use this sense of the ridiculous to break up the tendency toward a legal overload.

Capricorn Saturn: Saturn in Capricorn refers to the laws of maturation and manifestation. It represents the extent to which we may evolve or expand without becoming something else. Often it is understood as patriarchy, with the father as ruler. Ultimately we must realize that it actually refers to the scientific law that governs reproduction; every species reproduces its own kind—until it mutates into something else.

Both Saturn and Capricorn have long been linked ideologically to the past. In our childhood, our parents were our law. However, with the expanding awareness of today, those who look will discover that most maturing offspring achieve much more than their parents. In the personal coven, Saturn in Capricorn often represents the tendency to hold on to the parental laws—overtly out of respect, covertly out of fear. This holds us at a level of personal immaturity, often well into our adulthood. We are afraid to get too far away from home and the opinions and beliefs that were its laws.

The grace of this placement is that it requires us, by law, to succeed in society. We must function as adults in an adult world. This becomes the trigger point that Uranus can use to get us to move into our highest potentials. Capricorn Saturn is always the mark of a mature personality. All the change required is a change in consciousness. We may no longer think as children, but must think as adults, claiming our own authority to make our own laws.

Aquarius Saturn: Saturn in Aquarius once referred to a point which one might wish to achieve, but one beyond which we simply could not go. It was impossible. It was the boundary at the end of the world, mentioned in the Aries delineation. With the expansion of consciousness since the discovery of Uranus, it has become the law of possibility, or the law of evolution. We might say, then, that in the last two signs, Uranus is fully united with and immersed in Saturn, or Saturn in Uranus. They are no longer separate and related, but have become a single force for personal evolution.

This law opens the Capricorn limits, allowing us, when we have achieved the full possibilities of humanity, to become more than human. It allows us to achieve a real sense of meaning when we call ourselves the offspring of the Goddess. At the time this book was written, Uranus was in Capricorn and Saturn was in Aquarius. Together they opened the limits of what we can do and become. Perhaps most important of all, the practice of magic has been resurrected. Many are studying the old ways, seeking new applications based on what we have learned about the nature of consciousness. Magic and miracles are happening everywhere.

Saturn in Aquarius is the maxim that lies behind the idea that "hope springs eternal." Because we have hoped for what we thought impossible for so many centuries, the energy of all those hopes has combined and a magical event has occurred. We are the future; we dare not live in the past.

Pisces Saturn: Saturn in Pisces has long been regarded as the *law* of sacrifice and as a mandate to give up something of value for something else which usually has no personal value. It presumes to legislate a morality that outlaws logic in the name of faith. Uranus must then inspire us to examine the insanity of such a law. As we give up our faith in the laws of the past, and begin to claim our ability to set our own limits, we discover that the only *sacrifice* involved is the need to let go the past and make room in our lives for the future.

Ultimately, Pisces refers to mastery of activity that has been practiced long enough to function without conscious attention. It is something we can do without thinking about it. Only with the new awareness around the laws of consciousness, have we begun to realize that faith or trust must be derived from internal knowledge. We do know what we are doing, and how to do it. The unstated foundation of this is that at some point in our personal evolution we did learn such things, we did practice them, we do understand them, and by now we can do them automatically—unconsciously.

Saturn in Pisces has mastered the law in a way that allows us to function with the appearance of having no laws or limits. In reality, the real laws—meaning the rules of function—are inherent in our being. We do not need to think about them, and we do not. We merely go through life in our own unique fashion. It has been said that Saturn in Pisces always knows what it is doing even without realizing it, and even when it looks strange. In reality, this placement refers to the fact that the laws and limits of the strictly human no longer apply when we have begun to manifest our godhood. It is this ability to ignore certain limits which others take for granted that points most clearly to the fact that we are, after all, offspring of the Goddess.

To the extent that we become aware of this ability, to the extent that we learn to trust and take it for granted, we become the greatest magicians of the zodiac. Still, only those who watch closely are likely to notice. Knowing who and what we are, strange though our lives look to others, we do not think it strange at all.

URANUS: SATURN'S PARTNER

Historically, Saturn has been the Moon's partner. In our modern coven, the Moon is usually married to the Sun, so we are required to find Saturn a new mate. By default, we give him Uranus, she who has been displaced from her traditional role as mate to the Sun. Perhaps it is a sign of the times that even in astrology, divorce and remarriage has occurred. We find this pairing more meaningful than the original one. As Moon and Sun provide external leading for the coven, so Uranus and Saturn provide internal leading, as advisors to the High Priestess and Priest of the coven.

An old cliche states that necessity is the mother of invention. In our personal coven, Uranus represents this mother. The Saturn-Uranus pair represents the power of transcendence. It is Uranus' task to push, pull, or drag us beyond our Saturn limits so that we will not die of inertia. She will change our definitions if she can. Failing that, she will break up the routines of life, providing the necessary crisis to revolutionize our lives. If we do not bend, we break.

Saturn always represents the final goal, *as we know it.* Uranus defines our capacity for spiritual evolution, for personal mutation, for changing reality through knowledgeable use of the laws of consciousness. Each age represents a particular stage of growth in awareness that can and must be achieved in the general or mass consciousness. Their influence spreads across the lines of individuality, to society, to species.

The best illustration may be provided by looking at an individual. When a child is born, it has within itself all the inherent abilities needed to become a successful adult. However, because it lacks form, strength, judgement, etc., we set limits and boundaries on what it is allowed to do at different stages of growth. To the child, and at the time, these rules seem permanent and absolute. However, as the child progresses through ever higher levels of the maturation process, these rules are expanded and sometimes changed entirely.

Uranus provides the *exception to the rule*. Her principle applies across the human species. The age of Aries represented one level of spiritual maturation in the general population. The age of Pisces represented another. Each of these had its laws and limits. Avatars of the late Arian and early Piscean period were the heralds of the then-new possibilities for growth-in-consciousness, or spiritual growth. Even now the avatars for the next age are appearing. Discovering how consciousness works, we are no longer entirely subject to reality-as-it-has-been. We are learning to manipulate that reality, and to transcend the old limits.

Currently we are in the cusp period, in a bridging time, during which a few are mastering those things that will become the common heritage of the species during the next age. Many of us, as individuals, are important to the development of the next age, for we are expanding the possibilities for all. Modern Wiccans, along with certain other groups who essentially deal in what has traditionally been called magic, are forming the leading edge of change that will permeate the general consciousness during the coming age.

When we reach Saturn's limits, we have gone as far as we can go while remaining what we were expected to be by our family and/or society. Ultimately, Saturn represents the law of species that says that the offspring must resemble the parent. For a very long time Saturn was the outermost planet known to exist and he ruled both Capricorn and Aquarius as both the limits on the probable and the possible. Then, in 1781, with the discovery of Uranus, our solar system expanded. Simultaneously our concepts of civilization expanded, and the general consciousness was on its way. Most of the world had been colonized and the expansion of territory was reaching an end.

Life, by nature, must continue its growth. Uranus marked the beginning of exploration of mind and expansion of time. New inventions were superseded by newer ones, first to save time and then to fill the time created. Recently, some Uranian energy has begun to be redirected toward physical exploration and expansion as we turn our attention to space travel.

In the personal coven, Uranus, ruler of Aquarius, represents those persons or impulses that move us beyond the old Saturn (personal rules) and the limits of the Piscean age into the possibilities of Aquarius. She has the reputation of being a rebel and a disrupter but she will do that only if we are so resistant that crisis-activity is required. The value of crisis is that it often forces us to act without thinking. Studying our crisis behavior, we can discover forgotten abilities. When we wonder whether these abilities may not be so coincidental as we once thought, we are on the way to real mastery of them.

Uranus ever encourages us to own consciously and use the abilities that our unconscious lends us at times when our conscious mind cannot manage. She urges us to take the next step, to become more than we were. Whenever a phase is completed, whether it be growth in body, mind, soul, or spirit, Uranus urges us to move outward and upward, building on the Saturn foundations of the past. She reminds us that if we know how to build a log cabin we have learned the principles that will also build the Empire State Building.

URANUS IN THE SIGNS

Aries Uranus: Uranus in Aries points to our knowledge of survival, reminding us that life is eternal. If we will not see, she may use one or more health crisis to prove to us that we can survive anything—until we get it and call a halt to our poor health. How many of these crises it takes will depend on the "stubbornness" of Saturn. I once met an Aries man with Uranus in Aries who had survived sixty-one heart attacks. Surely that points to some uncommon knowledge about survival!

The grace of this placement is that, however long it takes, when our talent for survival becomes conscious, we can turn our attention to other things, pioneering in extraordinary and unusual ways. This man used his extensive knowledge of death to counsel terminal patients and their families.

Taurus Uranus: Uranus in Taurus points to our innate self-worth, reminding us that we are valuable to life. We have been taught specific rules about providing for our adult needs. Most of us learned that supplies are limited and that poverty is spiritual.

When beliefs about how to acquire money and/or how much we are entitled to have are too rigid, Uranus intervenes with crisis to remind us that we are always given what is necessary to survive, even when we lose control of our resources. She reminds us that no matter what the supply looks like or where it comes from, all supply comes from the source of life. She will teach us how to receive, and if we learn her lessons well, how to receive abundantly.

The grace of this placement is that when we recognize our value to life itself and learn to depend on life to supply us according to our value, the very floodgates of the Universe open. When and as much as we take supply for granted, as a given of our beingness, we will have all that we need and plenty to spare for others.

Gemini Uranus: Uranus in Gemini reminds us that we have the capacity to think and that we know how things relate. This commonly produces a mathematical mind that knows exactly where objects, people, ideas, etc., go and how much space must be maintained between them. Crises in the lives of these natives come from not applying this sense of internal order in their human relations.

Because they are sometimes accused of being cold and generally Saturnian, they may vacillate between too close and not close enough. Uranian crisis will then involve separation from or betrayal by siblings and/or neighbors that force us to seek families and friends of choice. We then have the opportunity to know the difference between blood-kin and kindred spirits.

The grace of this placement is that when we realize that we do know what place in our lives others should occupy and how close to allow them to be, we will begin to attract those people who have similar personal boundaries. This will give us a comfortable place for growth in other areas of our lives.

Cancer Uranus: Uranus in Cancer once pointed to the knowledge of flow. Now it usually directs us to the principle of momentum that says that anything in motion tends to remain in motion. More mundanely, this often refers to an unusual mother or family, suggesting the idea of inherited genius or insanity, and if Saturn is too strong, it will be difficult to get past these ideas without the added energy of crisis.

Cancer represents the idea of life as a growth process. If early childhood programming has limited the idea of growth too severely, our internal momentum may produce a crisis that will remove us from our home or from what represents the secure place to which we return when life becomes too much for us. It cuts off our line of retreat, forcing us to leave home and childhood behind. Saturn inertia collides with Uranian momentum and sometimes derails us, forcing us in a new direction. This provides the opportunity to begin trusting the growth process to take us where we need to be, with or without our conscious consent.

The gift of grace that this Uranus offers us is that life itself requires movement in consciousness and the very momentum of the learning acquired early in life is likely to carry us far into adulthood. It is, after all, a fail-safe system.

Leo Uranus: Uranus in Leo reminds us that we are the literal children of the Goddess. This placement may also be the origin of the statement, "Pride goeth before a fall." Leo often refers to a proud family that considers itself above certain people or activities. Such families may be so concerned with their reputation that they will curb any unusual talents that their children have on the grounds that they are undignified or unworthy of the family image, especially if Saturn is strong and fearful. Still, this Uranus must create something, and if not allowed to express in its inherent role, it will create a great deal of havoc until the Saturn ego boundaries lie in ruins.

The grace of this placement is that no matter how extensive those ruins, the coven can pick up the pieces, put them back together—often in new ways—to create a proper role and purpose in life. Awareness of these gifts can remove their destructive aspects and bring inspiration and invention to light and warm the world.

Virgo Uranus: Uranus in Virgo points out the nature and function of consciousness and how the outer form of life is shaped according to the inner purpose. All too often, Virgo becomes fixated on sacrificing the natural function of the body to some "higher service" and the result is that we work too hard with too little reward. Doing so, we may exhaust our physical energy, manifesting disease or injury.

When Saturn makes negative judgments on the body functions or the growth and maturation process of spirit, Uranus comes to our rescue. When he tries to separate them too sharply or to deny either, she creates a crisis that threatens the structure of life. This may be a health crisis, is often a career crisis, and usually is a crisis in consciousness. If it takes getting sick or losing a job to get the body stilled enough for us to listen, Uranus will say, "So be it."

The gift of this Uranus is the opportunity to realize that we are always given the perfect vehicle for the accomplishment of our chosen goal, and that, if we will listen, not even the loudest voices of family and society can drown out our inner guidance.

Libra Uranus: Uranus in Libra calls us to the consciousness of relationship and the peaceful acceptance of the principle of relativity. Libra longs for the quiet mind. Uranus in Libra reminds us that we know how to attain peace if we are willing to let go of our judgments. If Saturn's laws will allow us to recognize the principles of duality without making moral judgments on either polarity and if we can accept the need for both light and dark and their presence in life calmly, we can and will find peace and harmony in life. When Saturn insists on making moral judgments, Uranian crisis follows where we are most judgmental. That which we name harmful will harm us; that which we name good will be good to us. Uranus in Libra can mean a well-balanced and peaceful coven, or an unbalanced and noisy coven that may self-destruct. She compels us to weigh the value of following the inner leading toward the future against the effort required to remain fixated in the beliefs of the past.

The gift of this placement is the absolute knowledge that truth is, now and forever, relative to the level at which consciousness functions. When Uranus and Saturn are committed to coexistence, the result will always be harmony with the laws of life.

Scorpio Uranus: Uranus in Scorpio is a powerful force for change. Here Uranus and Saturn are fused and have become the law of transformation. When the Saturnian past is merged with the Uranian future, the force of change is directed into the present moment and something new is born out of something old. She is a powerful witch who becomes the secret power that infuses the work of the coven. She will usually not become active until mid-life, when the coven is beginning to stagnate and is danger of dying. Then she will appear, like a Phoenix rising from her own ashes, injecting new youth and life where age and boredom had threatened.

Her crises are often sexual in character; a new attraction may be just the tool for rejuvenating a middle-aged body. This may destroy the old marriage if it is no longer life-supporting, offering new opportunities that change the direction of life. She bides her time, waiting to present her gift, while power gathers behind Saturn's limitations. Then, when we need her most, she uses that power to transform our lives.

Sagittarius Uranus: Uranus in Sagittarius is the great expander who will literally burst the walls of our Saturn limitations, often with a guffaw of uproarious laughter. We might call this the placement of lucky accidents because it often produces crises that, after the fact, give us what we have long wished for, but almost never in the way that we expected.

This Uranus wants to overwhelm our limits, whether of physical, mental, emotional, or spiritual resources. She often shows us how much we can cope with, but this will always be relative to what we believe that we can have. To those who long for enlightenment and believe that the path to enlightenment goes through poverty and pain, Sagittarian Uranus' sense of humor may not seem so funny.

The gift of grace offered by this Uranus is the gift of laughter, and she will teach us to laugh no matter what it takes. From that day on, Saturn will never truly hinder us again.

Capricorn Uranus: Uranus in Capricorn is likely to take over your life at some point, for here she has all of Saturn's authority at her disposal. She represents, in almost pure form, the hopes and wishes of humankind to be more, to do more, than has been done before. She is the force of evolution trying to push us beyond our definition of humankind as a higher animal to that of offspring and heir of the Goddess. She must and will push us past the limits of our definition of self and of species. If it requires massive crisis to get us beyond our barriers of humility or self-consciousness, so be it.

She will push, pull, or drive us to be more than we believed was possible. She is the mother who insists that her child can do more, be more, become more than the family from which it comes. She is the wise teacher who knows that her own success will consist in producing pupils who exceed the limits of the teacher's knowledge. She reminds us that when any phase of growth ends, growth must be redirected into a new channel.

As this book was being written, the transit of Uranus through Capricorn produced a revolution in consciousness. Resistance from the religious right was triggered and society experienced outbreaks of violence in random places and contexts. A general, even global, crisis made it obvious to thinking people that something, somewhere must change before we destroy ourselves and/or our world. Perhaps the most critical modern events are those of children killing children, for these signify the future being used to destroy itself. Those whose judgmental thinking is contaminating the consciousness of children should notice that if the future goes, life does not merely stand still; it dies.

The gift of Uranus in Capricorn is her sense of responsibility and her ability to detach and step back far enough to see past the uproar and the pain. She knows what must be done if humankind is to continue growing, and she knows that when growth stops, death begins. More than that, she knows that the basic principle of life states that whenever a limit is reached, it is merely a signal that a new direction must be chosen. When the sea got full, life spilled onto land. When the land gets full it must move outward into the sky. As above so below; as in the universe, so in humankind. It is happening; this book is one proof of that.

Aquarius Uranus: Uranus in Aquarius carries in her hands, a new set of possibilities for the new age, and insists that we look past—not only our beliefs about what we can be, but also beyond our beliefs about what we can do. The story of a man who, about two thousand years ago, lived an extraordinary life doing extraordinary things has pervaded the general consciousness of the Piscean age. Only a few noticed that he is an archetype who represents the possibilities of what a human can do; the vast majority preferred to think of him as a god. We suggest that—whether he lived in form or merely in the subconscious areas of mind—he stands as the living representative of the parameters within which conscious development would take place during the Piscean Age. By the end of this age, the general definition of humanity must include abilities similar to his.

We might then refer to the presence of an Aquarian Uranus in the personal coven as that of the Goddess, herself, for she literally represents the presence of new creative possibilities. It is she who reminds us that the outer coven represents the inner one and that the source of all magic is the self-knowledge that we have. Like all crises, but more intensely so, this Uranian mother will force us to realize that we have creative abilities far beyond what the world around us believes to be possible. Change will seem to happen to us, and to the people in our lives, and we will be forced to recognize that we are the creative cause of those changes and to accept the responsibility for the changes we have made.

This new Uranus in Aquarius generation will be incredibly powerful, for they must cross boundaries that are hundreds, even thousands of years old. Still, they come with an absolute knowledge of how to detach from their feelings and do what is necessary to insure the future. It would be well for us to watch for them, and to do what we can for them. They, more than anyone born during the past eighty to eighty-five years, hold the future in their hands.

Pisces Uranus: Uranus in Pisces is a goddess of the sea. She brings changes from the very depths of the soul, letting them pour across the landscape of your life like tides on the seashore. The feeling of new knowledge available surges up, then back, bumping the barriers of consciousness, each time softening the boundaries and limitations of thinking a little more. Her mission is to teach us to trust the process of personal, social, and spiritual evolution, to allow ourselves to be something entirely different from we were taught to believe is possible.

If our Saturn limits remain too rigid, if they will not erode and dissolve, she will bring unconsciousness through some illness or accident that literally wipes much of the memory clean so that we can begin again. Those with this placement are the living symbols for the process in which the soul returns to Source, rests for a time in its gentle oblivion, and then emerges again into a new incarnational development.

This coven often seems to be at the mercy of outer circumstances beyond its control, circumstances which force a death and rebirth experience from which an entirely new coven emerges. The next generation, born at the bridging of the ages, will have great significance. These will surely bring dramatic change into the world through their own being. They will not settle for less.

NEPTUNE: THE SUBCONSCIOUS MASTER

Until Lady Uranus does her transcending work on Lord Saturn, our last couple remains nearly powerless and invisible in the coven. When Uranus opens the door to reality expansion, modern Wiccans will meet Lord Neptune, god of the vast oceans of consciousness and Lady Pluto, goddess of the world that lies beneath the surface of reality.

Once regarded with suspicion, this couple represented unknown aspects beyond traditional definitions of humanity. Humans habitually fear the unknown. Few pried into the mysteries and secrets of life. Ignored, rejected, and feared, these two planets have manifested in strange and difficult ways as they tried to get our attention.

Neptune was assigned as the "new" ruler of Pisces and given rulership over the idea that suffering is necessary to achieving sainthood. While we are more familiar with the Christian concepts of suffering saints and crucified Christs, the idea is also in the Yogi traditions. Eastern Masters often wandered the streets and roads carrying begging bowls, without a home or a bed. Behind these practices, lies the idea that the Earth, and life on it, is somehow contaminated and that to be *spiritual* we must seek to distance ourselves as far as possible from our desires. Because this notion is anathema to Wiccans, before Neptune can be admitted into the coven, new meanings must be found for him.

In traditional astrology, Neptune was connected with alcoholism, with *rose colored glasses*, day- and night-dreams and with the much-maligned abilities called imagination. Scientifically it symbolizes the second law of thermodynamics, proving that bounded completion predicts decay. In modern consciousness studies, we recognize the Neptune principle as a loss of individual form and cohesion with an accompanying reabsorption into the whole. Around Neptune, things dissolve and disappear from lack of attention. Equally, certain learned actions *dissolve into* beingness, becoming something we are, not something we do.[4]

Because we can only perceive objects with a vibratory level similar to our own, much of reality lies outside the awareness of our physical senses. When consciousness begins to rise, we may notice vague forms that are invisible to others around us. Simultaneously, other things may disappear, dropping beneath our attention level. Such phenomena are synchronous with a rise in consciousness.

Historically, individuals in the western cultures born with these super-wide or different perceptual bands were abused and condemned. Beliefs that only saints should do such things, and that these were nonexistent in the current reality, lead to excommunication from churches and society. Many created a socially acceptable disguise for Neptunian abilities by indulging in alcoholic spirits or other chemicals that produce similar effects. If one is under the influence, she or he can be excused much. Very often, residing in the same household with these Neptunians, were religion addicts whose *faith* obscured reason and allowed them to take pride in martyring themselves to a *Beloved Sinner*.

Many leaders in the consciousness movement are avowed recovering alcoholics and recovering addicts. These seed-beings carry the awareness of the vast oceans of thoughts, images, feelings available to human experience. When their *inherited* gods have abandoned them, the mutual support of *Anonymous* groups can help them to discover a new *Source of Power* that is more accepting of them. These groups call on the *Unknown Deity* who exists behind the symbols and images of their childhood religions. Their very name reflects the idea of hidden aspects behind and within reality.

More functional beings invested their visionary gifts in art work. Although artists live largely outside society, it accepts them. Many pictures and books have been *channeled* with-

---

[4]Abilities learned, practiced, understood, and mastered become the talents of later incarnations.

out the general consciousness taking note of it. Meanwhile, the resurrection of the ancient earth religions is helping humanity to get its feet back on the ground.

Synthesizing the ideas above, we see that the common factor in them is the ability to *tune in*, or focus on, different or greater aspects of awareness. More specifically, many are discovering or developing the ability to image, visualize, or envision as a creative act. The rose-colored-glasses of the religion-addict represent a dysfunctional application of this talent. Historically, the Neptune factor has often represented a negation of vision. It referred to *seeing less* or *blotting out*, rather than *seeing more* or intuition. Unwilling to change the picture, traditional Neptunians simply refused to see it.

Meanwhile, the Yogi-Christs of the east, some more ardent western saints, and the shamans of aboriginal cultures discovered that starvation, dehydration, and exposure could and did trigger altered states of consciousness. Generally, drugs and alcohol do not, but they do erode ego boundaries and release repressed areas of being. Natural abilities can then function beyond limited notions of rational man. Those who do not subscribe to artificial methods for changing the focus of consciousness have a wonderful opportunity to show a new way of joy and laughter, a way founded on our love of Earth and life on it.

Lord Neptune is the coven historian. He holds the memories, the *images*, of all past and future possibilities. Everything outside our current focus is in his domain. Through the inborn or learned ability of our Mercury/Fetch to *tune in*, or focus on both the invisible realities and the ordinary physical ones, consciousness becomes creative. When Mercury and Neptune cooperate, their combined information can be processed through Jupiter's computational abilities. Because it automatically expands our beliefs and releases judgment, ever larger portions of the vast ocean of Neptune's realm become accessible to human perception. A flow of cosmic energy/consciousness begins to pour into and through our lives.

In application, Lord Neptune brings us the element of faith or trust in personal, social, and spiritual growth, allowing the natural evolutionary process to take over. When we are focusing elsewhere, especially when Uranus is active in the coven, the natural law of obsolescence and dissolution[5] will allow the disintegration of obsolete boundaries. The Saturnian Ego may find itself *lost in a fog* or *going up in smoke*. Failing this, Neptune may bring unconsciousness through some illness or accident that literally wipes much of the memory clean so that we can begin again. Those with Saturn-Neptune contacts are the living symbols for the process in which the soul returns to the source, rests for a time in its gentle oblivion, and

---

[5]The second law of thermodynamics.

then emerges again into a new incarnational development. Notice that in northern latitudes Pisces occurs at the time of year when life begins to awaken from the long winter sleep.

Neptune-dominated covens may be at the mercy of outer circumstances beyond their control, with members wandering off in all directions in a sea of unconscious urges. Because their *trust factor* is so mature, current and future generations, born at the bridging of the ages, will have marked significance.

When Neptune functions with intention, we have the tools for conscious Plutonian magical work. Together they penetrate the mystery of creation. Out of the knowledge, power is born. Maturity's gift is creativity. What these covens believe about life and about themselves is what they will create and become. Woe to the society that convinces them that they are damaged, insane, or evil!

NEPTUNE IN THE SIGNS

Virgo Neptune: Neptune in Virgo refers to perfect trust. This was the first modern generation to have a complete *structural consciousness*. From it the evolutionary process emerged into world thought. During Neptune's transit of Virgo, Earth's population reached the *size* necessary for a significant rise in perceptual awareness. Those who preached the necessity of purifying the Earth's population generated wars. Their real intent was to prevent the process of human evolution that occurs when a *planetary consciousness* reaches a critical mass.

Virgo Neptune signifies the potential for discovery of process and method. It is the place from which we begin to practice for mastery. It begins at the mystery of puberty with all its stresses and choices to make. With practice, the potential of perfected form can and will unfold.

This generation has become the foundation for the movement into the Aquarian Age. They have learned to handle guilt without stopping their journey to the conscious awareness of their absolute perfection. The effect has been empowerment.

Libra Neptune: Neptune in Libra is the bridge between individualized consciousness and a return to mass thought. Born with one foot in the visible world and one in the invisible world, these natives are natural mediums. With both sides of consciousness awake for the first time, logic initially produced judgment. One part of consciousness was called *good* and the other *no-good*. They became spiritual beings that were "no earthly use" or physical beings "bound to earth" and filled with guilt. A few discovered their ability to act as mediums between physical and nonphysical reality.

Libra Neptune points out the relationship between the thinking Mercury-mind and the vast data-networks of the Universe. For a truly functional life, Mercury and Neptune must *marry*, learning to cooperate and share. This placement emphasizes the need for interaction between the right and left brains. This generation established the first species-wide contacts with the unknown world of spirit, opening the way for the intentional use of magical principles.

Scorpio Neptune: Neptune in Scorpio brought in the first generation of fully creative beings. Born with inner and outer senses[6] merged, their ability to penetrate the surface of life, showed them the creative potential of consciousness. Greater vision intensifies self-trust and trust in life. Out of this comes the ability to control their own reality by the power of their needs and desires. These are the new alchemists of life. They hold the power of life and death, and the power to create and destroy, inside them. Their only real enemies are the judgments held in the minds of the earlier generations who parented them.

Scorpio Neptune forces the integration of *ordinary logic* with the *extraordinary logic*, called intuition. To restate the thesis, this is the first entire generation born with the linkage between Mercury and Neptune fully established. If they try to separate logic and intuition, they create intense *fog* that can leave them lost and confused, unable to deal with the practical aspects of life.

This is the first generation born with a talent for turning thought into form, by intention. The logical and practical method for making their lives work is to use their perceptual function to *see* the way into the cosmic mind. When they *speak their word* from this position, creative activity follows immediately.

Sagittarius Neptune: Neptune in Sagittarius is the first generation of fully enlightened beings. The depth of consciousness reborn/remembered in the Scorpio generation expands horizontally in the Sagittarian generation. What was instinctive before, reached understanding during this transit. These natives instinctively understand the use of thought and word as a more effective tool than feelings and emotions. Because of it, they can call information from the invisible realms at will. When they learn to translate it into their native *language*,[7] their horizons expand in a conscious way.

Sagittarius Neptune is a *broad highway* that beckons the spirit to *higher ground*. More accurately, it shows absolute trust in the inner belief system. The wisdom of Sagittarius is its nat-

---

[6]Mercury and Neptune.
[7]The words and the way they learned to speak as children.

ural impulse to grow, to become something more. These are the first true mystics, aware that they carry the wisdom of the ages imprinted on their *DNA*. If the coven will forgive/give up the laws and rules of the past, it will go far in its quest to find the true meaning of life. Some seem almost to walk on air. Nearly all can astral travel at will.

Capricorn Neptune: Neptune in Capricorn is born at the highest level of awareness previously recognized in the definition of humanity. What was considered extraordinary in earlier generations is ordinary in these children. All are born with a fully matured consciousness, able to move successfully through multiple levels of reality. In a mundane world focused on physical survival issues, these must focus on the limits of form. They know instinctively what the *stress tolerances* of the human body are and they live at the outer limits of them. Most will, accidentally or purposely, push beyond the current definitions of the *possible* during their lifetimes.

The future of humanity depends on the reactions of adults who notice their abilities. Encouraged, they will transform the world. Discouraged, they may destroy it—not from intent but from their nature as fully creative beings. Here the abilities, developed since Neptune entered Libra, moved beyond thought into active demonstration, creating solid forms of reality. Whether their potential is used creatively or destructively is a matter of choice. Those who are currently parenting this generation are advised to be aware of the kind of choices these children learn to make, and the way they learn to choose. Woe to the adult who teaches a child that it is crazy or evil![8]

Aquarius Neptune: Neptune in Aquarius will dissolve the ego limits of the past, awakening the human spirit through its dream images. During this transit, hopes and fears held submerged in consciousness will emerge into physical reality, *popping up* all around us, even as they do in dreams. This includes the things we hoped would not happen, and those we hoped would happen. Remaining internal conflicts in the general consciousness will manifest in crisis so that we can see clearly how our thoughts and beliefs transform, transduce and transcend reality. What we understood about mastery in Sagittarius and proved in Capricorn, will become real knowledge. At that point we integrate it into beingness sufficiently to become the genetic inheritance of future generations.

Aquarius Neptune is the marker of cosmic consciousness. During this transit, the impersonal dreams of humankind will become its physical reality. What we *know* will be our experience, our truth, our future. This placement is about knowing our place in the cos-

---

[8]Take note of the occasional *explosions* of abused Indigos.

mic-universal plan. During this period, images of future possibilities will rise to the surface in the general consciousness and become creative. These covens would be well advised to, "Be careful what you wish for because you will certainly get it."

Pisces Neptune: Neptune in Pisces has come home. This is the mark of the *master's master*, who walks the world in an unconscious, unfocused, state, trusting its *instincts*. This transit will blur and obscure the limits of life because we have moved beyond the need for them. These covens will be barely visible to their antecedents because their *vibratory level* has risen to a *point of translucence*. They will look like ghosts to beings of lesser evolutionary development. During this transit, physical form—as currently defined—will become more illusion than real in conscious covens. Meanwhile, unconscious covens will revert to the animalistic state. These will be amoral, focused entirely on survival of the fittest.

Pisces Neptune takes life back to its essence. More literally it is exactly what it thinks and believes itself to be. It can live as a goddess, giving birth to life. Alternatively, it can *live* as a demon-destroyer of life, *giving birth to death*. Pisces is the Oureborus, swallowing its own tail. It is the beginning of the end AND the end of the beginning. The point between Aries and Pisces is the place where we choose the next cycle, *according to our perception of life*. Here, karma ends or begins again. Life goes forward or regresses. Morality dissolves into an undefined, fully potential state of becoming. Masters all, life makes no judgments on us.

Aries Neptune: Neptune in Aries refers to the birth of a new level of potential mastery. It brings a loss of distinctions because the Ego Image and the Self are unified. Divisions between body, soul, and spirit dissolve as the general level of consciousness begins a new phase. As currently understood, Aries will lose its survival issues in an absolute trust of life. To survivors born before the Neptune shift that occurred in the 1950s, this may be terrifying. Still, we think that most of those who would find it so will have left earth by then.

Aries Neptune is identified with its mastery of the previous level. It stands completed and ready for new evolutionary developments. During this transit a new vision and dream will surface from the subconscious memories of the human species. We see High Priestesses everywhere standing transfixed in ecstatic states while they give birth to the seeds of the future.

Taurus Neptune: Neptune in Taurus may have a major impact on health. The ultimate meaning of Taurus is integrity, and when Neptune dissolves integrity, only trust in natural law will hold life together. This generation will be charged with the integration of *new* consciousness into a structure of values that will support a less clearly defined world than the present one. When all is fluid and in motion, trust in the goodness of life will be a critical issue.

Taurus Neptune will *dream* or imagine the structures needed for the next evolutionary level of life. The values established in prior incarnations will formulate the reality of the current one. Intrusted with creating the *legal tender* of the Aquarian age, these covens will establish a network for focusing energy into significant ideas. In this way, they will *finance* the creation of greater worlds of experience.

Gemini Neptune: Neptune in Gemini may bring a loss of language as communication shifts into the telepathic level. Life will lose definition with the development of increasingly wide perceptual bands. When we can see with the naked eye what today's natives only perceive through microscopes and telescopes, the need for communication as we know it will disappear. The transit of Neptune through Gemini signifies *invisible communication*, or communication *at the speed of light.* When that happens, enlightenment will be so all-pervading as to exclude learning as we know it. Our current *need to learn* will blur out because it has become obsolete.

During this transit, every Fetch in every coven will become a clearing house or website for the vast Neptunian sources of intelligence. The outer perceptual function will be lost in the act of *tuning in* to universal *data bases.* When Neptune falls in Mercury's sign, he dissolves duality. Relationships will disappear in universal oneness and unions will become unified units of life.

Cancer Neptune: Neptune in Cancer will dissolve our security issues. Since most of these are based on fear of the unknown, a less physical, more conscious and enlightened society will be more aware of the natural flow of necessities through life. This will lead to total trust and comfort not unlike that experienced by a fetus in the womb. Cradled by our trust in life, we will be reborn into a new level of being.

No longer *higher animals*, we will feel our kinship to the Goddess at a gut level. Because we do, we will feel safe, secure, *at home*, in all circumstances. This placement will give birth to an entirely new type of coven consisting of *reborn* facets of being. Love, light, form, values, etc. will all have new meanings, *because* we have become a new species.[9]

Leo Neptune: Neptune in Leo will dissolve the *inherited role* of incarnate life, moving it into a cosmic performance level. No longer fully Solar Beings, we will take on Galactic citizen-

---

[9]More accurately, this is where life is reborn into a new level. In scientific terms we speak of a mutation.

ship. Here we claim our full inheritance from the Goddess of Life, apprenticing ourselves as full-time co-creators of the next reality.

Leo Neptune refers to active mastery—of life. The master-role is quite different from the old servant-role of the Piscean Age. This transit will clearly *shine a light on* or reveal our new galactic, maybe even universal, role. Here we take our place among the *Stars* or Monarchs of the Cosmos. Here we inherit the reality promised in the stars.

PLUTO: MOTHER OF REBIRTH

The Moon is our High Priestess and mother of life on this Earth. Lady Pluto is our Goddess of Transformation and the Unseen or the Underworld. She rebirths us to a galactic or cosmic heritage and citizenship. As our Moon is to us, Lady Pluto is to her. The Lunar Priestess is the womb of life on this earth. The Plutonian Priestess is the cosmic womb; i.e., the place from which we are born into greater than human form and consciousness, where every day, common, ordinary, logical living ends and unusual, uncommon, extraordinary, super-logical living begins. She is the great MOTHER of all magical and mystical processes.

When Lord Neptune's mastery brings any phase of experience to a culmination, the sum of all that has gone before is projected into seed form and becomes dormant. Whether we think of that phase as earth incarnations or an age, life goes comatose, awaiting the proper moment to begin the division and multiplication of cellular material that leads to a new form or formulation. Procreation symbolizes this process.

In recent decades we have developed relatively successful contraceptives. This made infertile sex practical—until the arrival of AIDS. Had we understood that our sexuality was designed as a natural spiritual ritual of creativity, AIDS and other sexually transmitted disease would not have been necessary. Blindly, humanity constructed a morality based on a combination of negative judgments about sex and a notion of sex as addiction. The result could only be something which used the creative energies of sex for the destruction of life.

The study of women's mysteries and of the dual-gender religions point to the answer that will heal the world. When we view human sexuality as a ritual for creating life, we can begin consciously to use our Uranus, Neptune, and Pluto energies to create at will. When we include all that supports human life in our definition of it, need, desire, even values as currently defined, will be fused into a powerful creative force. Only then will we become conscious co-creators and progenitors with our source.

That awareness represents the apex of human development as we know it. When knowledge is consciously directed into the invisible womb within our beingness, we create or procreate some form of life. The intentional and conscious use of spiritual knowledge produces spiritual form. As we recognize spirit in all forms, intention becomes power, giving us creative control over the form and direction of our lives. At this point Pluto becomes real to us.

A conscious coven will greet Lady Pluto joyfully in anticipation of a blessed event. When she inhabits a more primitive coven, they will dread and fear her as a source of nameless destruction. In her womb the invisible seed *dies* so that visible form can gestate. Our most important realization is that whenever Lady Pluto's womb is activated, the coven must and will go through a period of pregnancy and labor. We can regard that as a time of joy or a period of suffering. Attitude will determine how it feels. Pluto is the mother of all witches, both black and white, for in her resides the power of life and death.

When the planet Pluto entered human consciousness during the early 20th century, it heralded a major "growth spurt" in consciousness. It signified a rebirth of consciousness/energy. Being an infant, it correlated to physical infancy in that it grew rapidly. Appropriately it entered our awareness from Cancer, the place where any part of being is newborn, doubling and redoubling its "birth-weight," growing faster than it ever will again.

Pluto represents the power to reformulate our lives. A new life emerges from the energy-quantum of the former one, even as a butterfly was once a larva. Through the struggle we develop a new sense of self and being and we emerge triumphant. We who once *crawled in the dust* can now *fly to the stars*!

Before our coven entered life, Lord Neptune provided the seed and Lady Pluto provided the womb in which it was gestated. Out of this was born our personal Lady Moon and Lord Sun, even as we were born of our parents, and in a larger sense, of our ancestors. Before that, we were born of our race, our species, our God/Goddess.

Earlier generations had no real sense of the "parents before the ancestors." The awareness of our larger connections had to be reborn when the human species reached a level of maturity that could grasp it. Only when that knowledge became necessary and desirable, could it rise to the surface of human awareness. At the time of Pluto's *discovery*, humanity had achieved enough mastery over the environment to threaten the greater structures of life from which we emerged. Our sense of self clearly needed reformulation, so that we could use our inherent potential more creatively.

Appropriately, we are resurrecting the ancient earth religions at this time. The only thing that can save humanity from suicide is a return to love of Earth. Even as Lord Neptune seeds us with universal intelligence, so Lady Pluto gestates a rebirth into universal love/creativity. Together, this pair functions as "rebirthers" for the human spirit. Under their guidance we are changed from *destroyers of Earth's resources* to creators of the future. No longer *tied to Earth*, we can roam the universe on wings of light, selecting the alchemical elements that are the ingredients of the next universe/age.

The rebirth of Goddess worship heralds the rebirth of creativity at a new level. Reexamining our early belief systems gives us the tools needed for the creation of the next reality. Honoring both Lord Neptune as conscious mastery and Lady Pluto as magical creativity, we inherit the potential that lies within each coven.

PLUTO IN THE SIGNS

Cancer Pluto: In the Pluto in Cancer coven, the idea of spiritual heritage is reborn. When Lord Neptune dissolves our old ideas about the nature and meaning of life, the womb of life is cleansed and prepared for what will follow. In Lady Pluto's womb the scientific knowledge of genetics quickens the seed realization that we are "children of the Goddess." A successful pregnancy will give the coven a new self image and a new name, reflecting a deep realization of the meaning of rebirth.

Physically, this is reflected by the attention that child abuse is currently receiving. The source of that reflection was the abuse of trust by the fathers of many "Christian" churches who claimed the "father power" without taking responsibility for its proper use. Understanding that an abusive god threatens the survival of humankind, we revive a powerful life instinct. Realizing that living through destructive childhoods can only be the result of greater abilities than we have recognized in ourselves, we intuit our power. We are then, individually and collectively, reborn into the magical beings that we truly are.

Cancer Pluto empowers us to claim our spiritual genetics. Finally we can realize that the *Sons of the God* and *Daughters of the Goddess* can only be young versions of their parents. The offspring of the Creators must be creative. Reproductive offspring have themselves been reproduced by some copulative act. Every living thing reproduces its own kind. Gods and Goddesses are part of Life's structure. The reproductive principles apply to their children, grandchildren, great grandchildren, and the numberless generations that follow. The Children of Earth *are* the Children of Heaven, sinless and unflawed, true to their own nature. Here lie the seeds of the new metaphysics.

Leo Pluto: In the Pluto in Leo coven, the concept of spiritual rights is reborn. When Neptune dissolves our pride in self-motivation, nature takes over. In Lady Pluto's womb the seed realization of human rights quickens the idea that we are entitled to "inherit the kingdom." A successful pregnancy brings a new self-worth, reflecting the deep realization that we are loved and valued by the Goddess. Knowing that we are worthy of having more, we become willing to accept more, and our lives become increasingly richer.

A physical reflection is the widening gap between the poor and the rich and the decrease of the economic middle. In a world with the capacity to feed, clothe, and shelter itself several times over, the existence of starvation and homelessness is preposterous. It clearly shows that grandiose personalities who think that power equals the ability to manipulate other people are diverting creative energy for egocentric and unintelligent purposes.

Leo Pluto empowers us to act as agents for our Goddess. It is the power to act—as adults in an adult world. Still childlike, many of these covens *pretend* their way to positions of leadership in the community. This placement equals *willpower* at its most potent. Without *willingness-power* magical rituals can become dark and destructive. This coven *must* be willing to call down the Moon and Sun for guidance. Otherwise, pride will be its downfall.

Virgo Pluto: In the Pluto in Virgo coven, the concept of innocence is reborn from the ashes of *original sin*. As Neptune dissolves tradition, fertile ground is revealed. A successful pregnancy brings a new self-concept as perfect, whole and complete—created in the image and born from the womb of Pure Wholeness/holiness. No longer can the Children of the Goddess be controlled by guilt, struggling for some illusive ideal of perfection.

In Virgo, we emerge as fully individuated, ready for emancipation from our birth family. We must leave the past behind and begin to practice the skills we have learned there. It is the point where growth energy naturally shifts from the physical to the social. As Pluto crossed Virgo, psychology began to merge with the ancient esoteric spiritual traditions. During this period we developed or resurrected many rituals for releasing guilt and brought them into practice. The marriage of Pluto and Neptune, predicted a rebirth of humanity as more-than-man. A renewed interest in magic and mystery led millions to rediscover the Power of the Word when it is married to Faith/Trust in the nature of life.

Virgo Pluto empowers us to return to original perfection, to act from a state of innocence. Here we redeem the feminine principle (Eve) and return her power to her. Because she is free, she also frees her mate. United, male and female give birth to rising consciousness and the species called Man is returned to power on Earth. We are reborn as true genetic offspring of Goddess and God, perfect and pure, incapable of doing harm.

Libra Pluto: In the Pluto in Libra coven, the principle of rebirth reaches equality with the birth-principle. When Neptune dissolves the boundaries between physics and metaphysics, birth and death become equals in their roles as gateways to the future. Life and Death *marry* and form a union that gives birth to a greater future. The concept of a grace-filled universe arose from the ashes of eternal condemnation. Humanity was free to live in a more natural and spiritual way.

 As longer lifetimes and changing conditions dissolved the meaning of lifetime commitments, we released judgments. Many claimed the *rites of forgiveness* for their dying and destructive marriages and the divorce rate skyrocketed reflexively. No longer was humankind willing to live in the hell of dead marriages. New unions emerged from old relationships as people compulsively sought new meaning.

Libra Pluto empowers us to find peaceful solutions to our internal conflicts. The power is drained from judgement, allowing us the right to make fair and reasonable choices. Mistakes no longer call for life sentences. We can try and try again without fear of hellfire. The key realization is that simply moving the weight to the other side of Libra's scales solves nothing. The most powerful place is always the balance point at the center of the continuum.

Scorpio Pluto: In the Pluto in Scorpio coven, the concept of magic is reborn. When Neptune dissolved the control of old belief systems, knowledge about the power available through visualization, affirmation, and ritual rose to the surface of human consciousness. We began learning to control our own reality by reformulating our subconscious beliefs. Logic fused with intuitive mysteries, unlocking the secrets of the ages. Esoteric became exoteric and congregations took back their power from traditional priesthoods. Some call this a period of great destruction, but the only thing that died was obsolete thinking.

During Pluto's transit of Scorpio, sexual addictions raged in those who equated freedom of choice to a licence to behave in self-destructive ways. The ancient taboos won the first battle. Sexually transmitted disease raged across our awareness, seeming to prove the doomsayers right. Still, out of the chaos came new and potent techniques for mental and spiritual healing. AIDS became an arena where holistic medicine developed awareness of the role of human thought on health predicting success for the powers of Life.

Scorpio Pluto empowers us to greater vision and deeper understanding of the magic and mystery of life. It is the power to recognize and use the inner senses in cooperation with nature, with life. We become detectives, examining our taboos, discovering their causes. The subconscious begins to lose its mystery in the light of new developments in physics and metaphysics. Out of this, humanity is reborn to its natural divinity. Power is revealed as we realize that we are magical beings and that we *must* claim and love our power.

Sagittarius Pluto: The concept of enlightenment is reborn in the Sagittarius Pluto coven. When Neptune dissolved superstition and taboos, seed-realizations about personal power quickened the awareness of natural wisdom in Lady Pluto's womb. Where once humanity tried to compel and control Nature, we must now learn to cooperate with Her. Life is confronting us with our beliefs. At this writing, Pluto is moving across Sagittarius and we observe the role mass media is playing in producing epidemic health problems. When we believe that life or joy or pleasures are a cause of illness and death, life will prove it for us. Only as we learn to separate living truth from the malformed conceptions of traditional belief systems, can we avoid the destruction caused by negative thinking. The way our judgments rule our lives must be understood, forgiven, released. If not, the next age will be stillborn.

Sagittarius Pluto empowers wisdom and enlightens the world. Here we discover the meaning of our relationship to Earth and the Goddess. Here we learn the true meaning of life on Earth. When our understanding of life no longer fits into the old forms, we will formulate new ones from them. Bursting the bonds of Earth, we become citizens of the galaxy, both literally and symbolically. Sagittarius Pluto is the *warp drive* that will take us to new times and places. Woe to us if we take old judgments with us. We must live with, or die by them.

Capricorn Pluto: In the Pluto in Capricorn coven a new definition of humankind must emerge from the old, like a butterfly from a chrysalis. If humanity is to survive, we must take responsibility for redefining and redesigning our species. We must allow Neptune to dissolve the laws and traditions of earth-bound consciousness into the substance required for a new galactic species. *Homo-Aquarius* will be as different from homo-sapiens as butterflies are from larvae. They may not even recognize their common origins.

For some time each generation has been taller than the last. Recently we notice a much greater tendency toward obesity in the general population. Perhaps this is simply the prelude to physical transformation or mutation in the human species. Many of us have been conditioned to have negative responses to the idea of physical evolution in our own species. Still, if human consciousness outgrows the current version of physical expression, it must mutate or die. The lesson of Capricorn is always about recognizing boundaries as temporary *safety nets*, designed to protect us during periods of growth. As Pluto moves across Capricorn, Neptune will dissolve the limits of transformation so that we can go beyond all that we have hoped or dreamed.

Capricorn Pluto empowers us to take our place as the true genetic and legal heirs to the Goddess. In this arena, *inheritance* will take on new meaning, as our species is redesigned to fit galactic models.

Aquarius Pluto: Pluto in Aquarius covens will invent new possibilities. When Lord Neptune has resolved all human hopes and wishes into the substance of new creation from Lady Pluto's womb, new hopes, new wishes, must be formulated. It is always our hopes for the future, our wishing that we could, that pull us forward into new evolutionary states. A new species must have new goals, hopes, and dreams. If it does not, it will be stillborn.

This generation may see much chaos as the young gods and goddess who then inhabit Earth play with their re-creative powers. Their goal will be that the entire Earth becomes *new and improved.* Those of us who have lived through a significant portion of the industrialization of Earth have seen that not all innovative *improvements* truly are that. This period will be one of trial and error leading to great upheavals. When an entire young species can move mountains and play with the weather, rebel spirits must learn to contain their exuberance. Still, by this time, interplanetary travel will be practical so those who wish to, can leave the eruption of co-creative activity behind.

Aquarius Pluto will give unprecedented powers of life and death over Earth, herself. Some of us remember the fears experienced by many when atomic and plutonium bombs entered reality. The transit of Pluto across Aquarius is likely to create just such fears in the remaining unevolved populations of Earth. By that time, these will be in the minority, even as the true Aquarians are now. Many will flee to other worlds, even as Europeans and later Asians fled to the then *new world* that we know as the United States of America.

Pisces Pluto: In the Pluto in Pisces coven, the last vestiges of *homo sapiens* will blend into the new reigning species on Earth. Gradually Earth will regain her balance as the once *new and extraordinary* abilities become integrated into a state of ordinariness. Earth will look different, humanity will be different, and the differences will go unnoticed.

As Pluto moves across Pisces, the new species will forget the old, losing their memories of *homo sapiens*. All the *talents* of the late Piscean age will be normal attributes of the species homo-Aquarius. All that was once supernormal will be the accepted norm, and life will move into a state of *grace* that some of our readers would think boring. It will be as though humanity has nowhere else to go.

Pisces Pluto empowers the kind of peace that we call Nirvana. The entire coven will have become *spiritualized* to a high degree, knowing its own perfection and purity. In pristine clarity it will live in a state of limitlessness. The image bears a striking resemblance to esoteric descriptions of periods that exist between incarnations. This is true Heaven on Earth. Some would call it the End of Time. Technically, it is the end and fulfillment of the Piscean Age.

Aries Pluto: Then dawns the Age of Aquarius. Pluto in Aries covens will be seeded, broadcast across the galaxy. All the best and worst of Earth will be invested in new planetary communities. Whatever evolutionary state incarnating spirits want, will be available. Reborn humanity will not only produce butterflies and angels, but a few horseflies, moths, millers, and some dragons.

Those beings who fled Earth to avoid the natural evolution of the species will colonize new worlds, during the Pluto in Aquarius phase. These civilizations will begin only slightly ahead of the original Earth colonies, and with adverse conditions, some will regress before they begin to evolve. Highly evolved beings who can formulate bodies from natural elements will colonize other planets. These will adapt well to conditions, and most will begin a new phase of development in consciousness. Earth governments may deport rebellious spirits to planets more suitable to their talents.

Aries Pluto empowers the human "I AM." This is the conception point of the next phase of human development and where the next age truly begins. Many *Seed-Covens* will be variations on the present ones. The various *Star Trek* conceptions represent this type of reality.

Wherever Aries activates, something entirely new is born. Somewhere in the galaxy an entirely new version of conscious life will emerge. We cannot conceive of what this will look like or be. The time is not yet. The period from Capricorn through Pisces must always be complete before Aries can be conceived and born from its undifferentiated substance. Consequently, our delineation of Pluto ends here.

We have not attempted to predict the transits of Pluto across Taurus and Gemini because they will take many forms. Their names will be legion. Each colony seeded will have its own form and consciousness, shaped by the local conditions. These are the signs of differentiation. Here life divides into physical and nonphysical and various grades of consciousness invest themselves in these forms. This will be a time when Life begins again, starting on a new path of evolution. We cannot predict this from our present base in consciousness.

Conclusion

We have designed this book to entertain our audience. Specifically, it is directed toward stimulating active minds to draw their own conclusions and make their own predictions. If the past is mother to the future, the things we can imagine and dream will be the reality of the next phase of human development. Some readers will find this stimulating. Some may find it horrifying. There is room for all.

Blessed be the Mother and her Consort. Blessed be the Child.
Co-creators all, we are the magicians
who will create the future.
So mote it be.

www.ingramcontent.com/pod-product-compliance
Lightning Source LLC
LaVergne TN
LVHW061300060426
835509LV00013B/1502